365

ART & CRAFT
Activities

Rita Hoppert, Ed.D.

Illustrated by Jim Connolly

pil

Publications International, Ltd.

Louis Weber, CEO
Publications International, Ltd.
7373 North Cicero Avenue
Lincolnwood, Illinois 60712

ISBN-13: 978-1-4127-1662-8
ISBN-10: 1-4127-1662-4

Manufactured in China.

8 7 6 5 4 3 2 1

Rita Hoppert, Ed.D., is an educational writer and consultant who has worked with children for over twenty years. She has been a contributing editor to *SPARK! Magazine for Children* and the program director for a family literacy program.

Contributing writer: Donna Shryer

Illustrator: Jim Connolly

Contributing illustrator: Yoshi Miyake

Cover illustration: George Ulrich

Frisbee™ is a registered trademark of Wham-O Manufacturing.

CONTENTS

INTRODUCTION

365 Art & Craft Activities sounds like a huge number of projects to interest your children and to keep them busy for many hours. But the process of making art and craft projects is more than just busy work. In each activity, children learn new skills. They learn responsibility for their materials and how to clean up after themselves. They learn creative thinking skills as they combine a new idea with another. They learn to control the eye and the hand not only for art's sake but also for necessary school skills. And they increase their attention span, too.

This book encourages skill building through projects. It is divided into five chapters—arts, crafts, crafts to share, year-round projects, and hobby crafts. Each project includes a list of what you'll need and easy-to-follow instructions. Take the time to go over the instructions carefully with your child. Each project has been rated with a challenge level: easy, medium, or challenging. Hand symbols near the title of each project represent the degree of difficulty: Three hands indicate projects requiring advanced skills, two hands symbolize intermediate skills, and one hand signifies projects using basic skills.

While many projects fit one category, some processes cut across chapters; for example, papier-mâché is introduced in chapter 1, but it's also used to make a piñata in chapter 3. Cut-and-paste skills are part of almost all the chapters. Another crossover theme is an adult's supervision of children's play. Kids need help with some projects, such as baking in an oven. Other projects require only a watchful eye. You know your child. A five-year-old needs more supervision than a 12-year-old, but even within one age, two children may require different amounts of monitoring.

There are some tools that are necessary for many projects throughout the book as well—a paper supply, glue, paints, and an art smock.

• Paper: There are many places to find scrap paper for the majority of projects. Computer paper, junk mail, and boxes are just three ideas. However, some projects call for specialty papers. School supply stores carry newsprint, poster board, and construction paper.

• Glue: Most projects call for craft or white glue. It is a water-based glue that can be thinned for easy application. Fabric glue, which is not water-soluble, holds up outdoors or in projects that will be washed.

• Paint: There are many types of paint. A watercolor paint box is an easy, storable, and quality paint application. Poster paint is a tempura paint that comes in powder form or premixed in squeeze bottles. (An empty egg carton works great as a paint box.) Water-based acrylic paint is a vibrant form of paint that can be used on all surfaces. It dries permanently, but when wet is easily cleaned up with water. Make sure your children clean painting tools thoroughly when they are finished painting.

• Art Smock: Make sure your child wears a smock to protect clothes while working with paints and other messy materials such as clay or plaster. See the Paint-Proof Art Smock on page 234 to make a protective apron. Encourage your child into a routine for its use!

This should be an enjoyable, creative experience for both you and your child. Encourage your child to create their own versions, using their own ideas. Enjoy your time together, have fun, and admire the lasting results!

ART PROJECTS

Chapter 1 probably has the most "exotic" techniques in the whole book. But you'll quickly demystify projects like batik and papier-mâché once you get started. To help the process along, preread the instructions with an adult. Be sure to check the materials list to see if all items are available. Some of the projects involve the use of art materials such as polymer clays, water-based acrylic paints, and a brayer. Make sure you wear an art smock or an old shirt when working with any messy materials. When working with plaster, always mix it in a disposable container. Do not pour unused plaster down the drain; throw it away.

ANIMAL COMBOS

Mix and match animal features and colors to draw the most unusual zoo in the world.

What You'll Need: Old magazines or books, tracing paper, black felt-tip pen, drawing paper, colored pencils

Find pictures of 2 different animals that are about the same size. Place a piece of tracing paper over one animal, such as a giraffe, and use a black felt-tip pen to trace the head and neck. Then place the tracing paper over the other animal—perhaps a fox—and trace the body and legs. You've just created a giraffox!

Place a sheet of drawing paper over your tracing paper, and trace the giraffox. Using colored pencils, give your giraffox a wild coat. Add feathers, fur, horns, or tails of other creatures to make your animal look even more different. Use this drawing technique to create all kinds of original animals. Think of combinations to make the most ferocious, the fastest, or the most colorful creature.

CLAY POCKETS

Create this special pocket to put on a wall, hang as a Christmas tree ornament, or hide tiny treasures in.

What You'll Need: White polymer clay, rolling pin, waxed paper, toothpicks, craft knife, items such as keys, coins, or buttons (to make impressions in clay), drinking straw, aluminum foil, acrylic paints, paintbrush

Roll out a ¼-inch-thick layer of clay, on waxed paper. Use a toothpick to make the outline of a 5-inch-diameter circle (the back piece) and a 2½-inch half circle (the pocket) in the clay. Cut both pieces from the clay (have an adult help you with the craft knife). If you want to decorate your clay pocket, press some small items in both clay pieces, or use a toothpick to make tiny impressions, such as baseball stitching.

Place the half-circle pocket piece over the back piece and pinch the edges together. Then use the straw to punch a hole at the top. Place a piece of crumpled foil into the pocket to hold it open while it dries. With an adult's help, bake clay according to package directions. Once it has cooled, paint with acrylic paints.

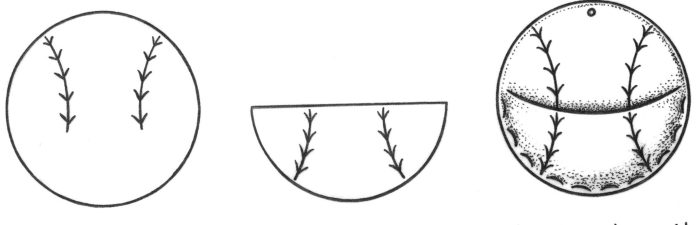

back   pocket   pinch clay together

IRONED COLLAGE

3

This project re-creates a stained glass effect, and it looks especially pretty when you hang it in a window.

What You'll Need: Plastic sandwich bag; collage items such as colored tissue paper, doilies, glitter, and tinsel; iron and ironing board; aluminum foil; clean, old towel; needle and thread

Arrange colored tissue paper, doilies, glitter, tinsel, and any other thin, flat items in a design or pattern inside a plastic sandwich bag. Overlap different colors of tissue paper to create new color combinations, sprinkle glitter to add sparkle, and create flowers with doilies. Seal the bag shut. Then place the bag between 2 pieces of aluminum foil. Cover with an old towel. With an adult's help, iron the "sandwiched" bag for about 15 seconds. The bag will melt and hold your collage in place. After the collage has cooled, poke a hole in the top center of the bag with a needle. String it with thread to hang it in a window.

STILL LIFE PICTURE

4

You can bring old wallpaper samples to life by layering different patterns, shapes, and colors on one background.

What You'll Need: Wallpaper scraps or old wallpaper books, scissors, poster board, craft glue

Here's a great way to use leftover wallpaper. (If you don't have any wallpaper scraps, you can get old wallpaper books at a home decorating store.) Have an adult help you cut "still life" shapes such as a table, a bowl, and fruit from different patterns of wallpaper scraps. Now set up your "still life" scene on a piece of poster board. You can leave the poster board plain or glue a sheet of wallpaper over it to create a wallpapered background for your "still life" scene. Place the wallpaper table on the poster board background, then put the bowl shape on top of the table, and add the fruit shapes in the bowl. Once you've arranged the pieces, glue them in place.

PAINTING IN OPPOSITES

5

Every color has an opposite or complementary color. Use the opposite color of what's expected and create a surprising world.

What You'll Need: Pencil or colored pencils, drawing paper, ruler, newspaper, watercolor or poster paints, paintbrush

Do you know which colors are the primary colors? They are red, blue, and yellow. Which colors are the secondary colors? Mixing the primary colors creates the secondary colors. They are green, orange, and purple. Now that you know which colors are which, draw a color wheel. To create a color wheel, draw a circle on a piece of drawing paper. Use a ruler to divide it into 6 equal "pie" pieces. Label or color in every other "pie" piece as a primary color. Then fill in the opposite secondary colors. Label the "pie" piece opposite of red as the secondary color green. Finish labeling the remaining colors.

Cover your work surface with newspaper. Draw a summer scene of a field with flowers and trees. Paint it in opposite colors. Use your color wheel to pick the opposites. For example, your grass will be red, and the sky will be orange with a purple sun. Let the paint dry.

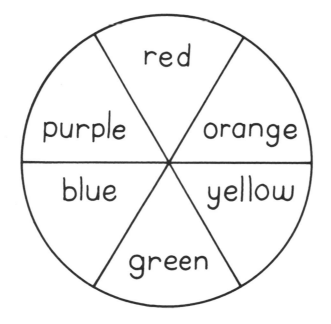

6 CRAZY PUTTY DOUGH

With this putty dough, you can make all sorts of silly shapes or magically lift pictures off the funny pages.

What You'll Need: ⅓ cup liquid starch, baking sheet, 1 cup craft glue, craft stick or small spoon, newspaper comics, drawing paper

Pour liquid starch on a baking sheet. Using a craft stick, slowly stir in craft glue. After it starts to clump, let the mixture set for 5 minutes. Dab a small amount of starch on your fingers and knead the mixture. Now you can pull it, roll it, and stretch it—just like putty!

As you experiment with your homemade putty, use the baking sheet as your work surface. (Be careful not to get it on the carpet or furniture.) Use the putty to make prints of your favorite comics. Press it on the comic strip, peel it back, and then press the putty on a piece of paper. When you're finished playing with the putty, store it in a small airtight plastic container.

CHALK IT 7

It's incredible how one piece of pastel chalk creates two different colors when you draw on wet paper and then on dry paper.

What You'll Need: Sponge, pastel chalk, construction paper, hairspray (optional)

Lightly dab a moist sponge on one half of a sheet of construction paper to dampen it. Draw a design on both the wet and dry halves of the paper with pastel chalks. Make a squiggle picture by drawing a continuous curvy line all around the paper. Add more squiggles, and color in the spaces. Now compare the colors on the wet and dry surfaces of the paper. When the paper dries, have an adult seal the picture with a fine mist of hairspray.

8 SPECIAL-SHAPE CASTINGS

Use silver foil to form gold-medal designs that you can give as gifts or keep just for yourself.

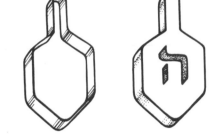

What You'll Need: Newspaper, heavy-duty aluminum foil, ruler, plaster of paris, spoon, acrylic paints, paintbrush

Cover your work surface with newspaper. Use a sheet of foil to create a mold for your plaster casting. Shape the foil into a star, a dreidel, or the design of your choice. Fold the foil edges up to create a 2-inch rim around the shape. Smooth out any big folds with your fingers. Have an adult help you mix the plaster of paris according to the package directions. Carefully spoon the plaster into the mold. Let it set. Once the plaster has dried, pop the casting out of the mold. Paint it using acrylic paints.

9 FINGER PAINTS #1

Find tools that imitate nature's own textures. A sponge makes a great tree trunk. A comb makes super ocean waves.

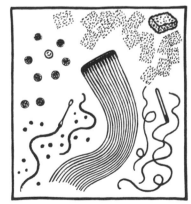

What You'll Need: Newspaper, mixing bowl and spoon, warm water, 1 cup soap flakes, small containers, food coloring, tape, finger-paint paper, painting tools such as a comb, cotton swab, craft stick, and sponge

Cover your work surface with newspaper. Place soap flakes in a mixing bowl. Slowly stir in small amounts of warm water until the mixture is thick like pudding. Spoon mixture into separate containers. Stir in a few drops of food coloring in each container.

Tape a piece of finger-paint paper down on your work surface. Spoon some finger paint onto the paper and use your fingers and hands to swirl it all over. Blend the colors—especially red, yellow, and blue—to make new ones. Use the painting tools to scratch designs in the paint. Experiment with other types of paper, too. Try finger painting on foil, cardboard, and even plastic wrap.

10 SAWDUST CLAY DOUGH

Bet you thought sawdust was garbage! With this project, you can turn sawdust into wonderful bowls, vases, and even puppets.

What You'll Need: Newspaper, 3 cups sawdust (available at a lumberyard), 2 cups wet wallpaper paste (mix with water according to package directions), acrylic paints, paintbrush, large bowl and spoon, tube, wire frame, or foil

Cover your work surface with newspaper. Have an adult help you mix the sawdust and wet wallpaper paste together in a large bowl, and stir until the mixture becomes doughlike. Take the sawdust mixture out of the bowl, and knead it with your hands.

Use this thick clay to make textural sculptures with an adult's help. You can form your sculpture over a tube, a wire frame, or a small ball of foil. This clay is also great for making small bowls and vases. Once you've finished shaping your clay creation, paint it with a coat of wet wallpaper paste to set it. Let it air dry for about 4 days. When dry, paint it with acrylic paints.

SALT & WATERCOLOR PICTURE 11

Salt is great on popcorn, but did you know it's also fun to sprinkle it over a wet painting?

What You'll Need: Newspaper, pencil, drawing paper, watercolor paints, paintbrush, salt

Cover your work surface with newspaper. Sketch a picture, such as a panda bear in a forest, on a piece of drawing paper. Paint the drawing using watercolor paint. While the paint is still wet, sprinkle it with salt. Let it dry. The painting will take on a textured look, and the paper may even crinkle and pucker. You can use this painting technique to make textured backgrounds for holiday cards, stationery, and more.

TOOTHPICK SCULPTURE

12

You need patience and a steady hand to create these toothpick designs, but the effort is well worth it.

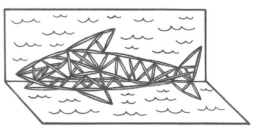

What You'll Need: Waxed paper, flat, round, or colored toothpicks, craft glue, blunt scissors, blue construction paper, crayons or markers

Cover your work surface with a sheet of waxed paper. Glue toothpicks together to make a skeleton shape of a shark. Dip the toothpick ends in glue; then glue each toothpick together piece by piece. After you've created the base of the shark, fill in the body with long and broken toothpicks until the shape is rounded. Then add fins and a tail. Let the glue dry. Now make a display stand for your sculpture. Fold a piece of blue construction paper in half lengthwise. Draw on some waves. Glue the shark to the paper.

SCULPTING CLAY DOUGH

13

Ever wondered what a yellow elephant looks like? Or a purple spaceship? Find out when you sculpt and paint your wildest fantasy.

What You'll Need: Saucepan, 1 cup cornstarch, 2 cups baking soda, 1¼ cups water, waxed paper, poster paints, paintbrush

In a saucepan, mix cornstarch, baking soda, and water. With an adult's help, heat it on a medium setting. Stir the mixture continuously until it thickens. Let it cool.

Place a sheet of waxed paper over your work surface. Knead the clay dough for a few minutes. Roll the clay into a ball, and shape it into small sculptures. Pinch ears and legs to make bears, bugs, and bunnies. Let the figures air dry, then paint them using poster paints.

You can also use this homemade clay for the Sculpting Clay Statues project on page 67—just let it air dry instead of baking it. If you want to play with the clay another day, store it in a sealed plastic bag or an airtight container, and keep it in the refrigerator.

FRAMED ART

14

This project gives your artwork a finishing touch. You'll be just like a professional artist in a real gallery.

What You'll Need: Precut colored mat (available at art supply stores; find the size to fit your artwork), magnetic strips, craft glue, assorted shapes of dry pasta, curly paper (see Curly Paper Art on page 162), or assorted colors of glitter and sequins

Decorate the mat with assorted shapes of pasta, curly paper, or glitter and sequins. Glue them on the frame in a random design; let the glue dry. Cut 4 pieces of magnetic strips and glue them to the back of the mat. Use this decorated mat to display your drawings on the refrigerator. Change your picture as often as you like.

SHADOW PUPPETS

15

Even with all the lights on, these funny shadow shapes stay around to play some more.

What You'll Need: Drawing paper, masking tape, pencil, colored pencils, crayons, or markers, scissors, craft glue, poster board or cardboard, craft stick

Pick out a room with a light-colored wall. Turn on a lamp. Practice making shadows on the wall with your hands. Cross your thumbs over one another and spread your fingers apart to make a bird. Or hold one hand sideways with your thumb sticking straight up on top and your pinky separated from your other fingers at the bottom to make a dog.

When you're done practicing, tape a piece of paper on the wall. (Don't press the tape too hard or leave it on too long—you don't want to remove any paint or wallpaper.) Make a shadow puppet on the paper, and have a friend draw an outline around the shape. Use household items such as gloves, strainers, and staplers to make more shadow puppets. Take turns with your friend making shapes and drawing outlines until you have a whole zoo. Color in your animal shapes.

To make your shapes into stick puppets, cut out an animal shape, and glue it on a piece of poster board or cardboard. Cut around the shape, and glue a craft stick to the back.

FOAM TRAY CASTING

16

Look around your house for small, flat objects, and reproduce their shape to make paperweights and pretty plaques.

What You'll Need: Newspaper, plaster of paris, clean foam food tray (from fruits or vegetables only), tools such as a craft knife, cookie cutters, keys, and screws (to press in foam tray), paper clip (optional), acrylic paints, paintbrush

Cover your work surface with newspaper. Use a craft knife (adult use only!), cookie cutters, keys, and other objects to carve and press shapes in the foam food tray. Press objects in a design or a picture. To create more detail in the plaster, press hard into the foam. Be careful not to cut all the way through the foam.

Have an adult help you mix the plaster of paris according to package directions. Carefully pour the plaster in the foam tray. (Be sure to throw unused plaster away. Do not pour it down the sink; it will clog the pipes.) If you'd like to hang your plaster casting, press a paper clip into the top edge. Let the plaster set. When it's dry, pop it out of the tray. Add color to your plaster casting with acrylic paints.

RUBBINGS

17

It seems like all you're doing is moving a crayon back and forth. Then almost like magic, an object appears.

What You'll Need: Drawing paper, leaves, crayons or colored pencils

Place a piece of paper over some leaves. Rub a crayon back and forth over the paper to show the texture of the leaves. Use this technique to experiment with other textures. Use paper and crayons to rub over textured surfaces around the house such as wood floors, tile, or bulletin boards. Greeting cards with raised designs also make great rubbings. Mix and match textures on one piece of paper to create a textural collage.

COILED BOWL

18

This is truly a bowl of a different color, and it becomes extra special when you make it yourself!

What You'll Need: Assorted colors of polymer clay, waxed paper, blunt scissors, aluminum foil, ovenproof bowl (about the size of a salad bowl), craft knife

Using the palms of your hands, roll clay on waxed paper to make 9 to 10 rolls of clay about 10 inches long. Then roll each clay piece into a circular coil. Cut a circular piece of foil slightly larger than the bowl. Place coiled clay pieces on the foil close together like puzzle pieces. Use your fingers to smooth the surface of the coils until the clay blends together. (Dipping your fingers in water helps to smooth the clay.) Make sure there are no gaps between the pieces. Ask an adult to use a craft knife to trim edges if necessary. Turn the bowl upside down, and turn the clay sheet over onto the bowl. Press into place. With an adult's help, bake the bowl according to package directions. After the clay has cooled, remove foil and bowl from clay.

DOUBLE DRAWING

19

You may think you're seeing double, but you're not. You're seeing a colorful design drawn with two crayons at once.

What You'll Need: Masking tape, crayons, colored pencils, or markers, drawing or construction paper, watercolor paints and paintbrush (optional)

Hold 2 crayons, colored pencils, or markers side by side and tape them together. You can tape together two of the same color or two different colors. Draw a picture on a piece of drawing paper. Your picture will have double lines. Write your name a few times or make the same design, such as a heart, over and over in different colors and sizes. Change color combinations often. After you've finished drawing your picture, color the space in between the lines to create a bold design. If you use crayons to draw your picture, color it in using watercolor paint to create a resist effect.

MODELING CLAY DOUGH

20

It's amazing how many interesting shapes you can make with this colorful and fun clay dough.

What You'll Need: 1½ cups flour, ½ cup salt, 1 tablespoon vegetable oil, ½ cup water, mixing bowl and spoon, waxed paper, food coloring

Mix flour, salt, oil, and water together in a big bowl until the mixture becomes doughlike. Place a sheet of waxed paper on your work surface, and sprinkle it with some flour. Knead the clay dough into a ball on the floured waxed paper. Divide the ball into separate lumps of clay, and add some food coloring to each. Knead each lump well again. Now you can sculpt the clay dough into any shape you want. When you're done sculpting, you can leave your clay creations out to air dry, or store the clay in separate plastic bags or airtight containers. Keep them in the refrigerator until the next time you play.

PAPIER-MÂCHÉ MASK

21

Build an original mask out of newspaper strips, and hang your artwork on the wall.

What You'll Need: Newspaper, stapler and staples, flour and water (for paste), measuring cup, mixing bowl and spoon, 1×4-inch newspaper strips, masking tape, scissors or craft knife, acrylic or poster paints, paintbrush, acrylic sealer (optional)

1. Cover your work surface with newspaper. Fold several sheets of newspaper into long bands. Using the illustration as a guide, make a mask frame (an oval half) with bands of newspaper stapled together.

2. Mix flour and water together to make a paste. Use 1 cup of flour for each cup of water. Blend until the paste is smooth. Dip a strip of newspaper in the paste. Rub the strip between your fingers to remove any extra paste. Put the strip over the mask frame and smooth in place. Repeat until the mask is covered with 4 or 5 layers of strips. To add more dimension to your mask, tape on projections before you add the last layer of newspaper strips. Use paper rolls or cones for horns, ears, and a nose. Let the mask dry overnight.

3. With an adult's help, cut out the eyes and a mouth. Paint the mask and let it dry completely. To make your mask shiny, apply a coat of acrylic sealer.

Mask frame

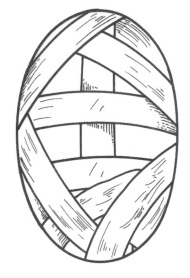

BIG BRUSH ART

22

All the best artists know that sometimes an unusual paintbrush creates the most remarkable picture.

What You'll Need: Large cardboard box, scissors, newspaper, 1-inch paintbrush or foam brush, poster paints

With an adult's help, cut out a large panel of cardboard. Cover your work area with newspaper. Paint a painting on your cardboard "canvas" using a 1-inch paintbrush and poster paint. Illustrate something big such as a skyscraper, the Grand Canyon, or even a Ferris wheel. You can also paint something that is small on a large scale. Try filling the whole space with one autumn leaf or a bouquet of sunflowers.

POINTILLISM PICTURE

23

Many famous painters have used this technique: They paint a picture using lots of dots to create solid shapes. It's amazing but true!

What You'll Need: Newspaper, old magazines, blunt scissors, craft glue, drawing or construction paper, cotton swabs, watercolor or poster paints

Cover your work surface with newspaper. Find a colorful picture in a magazine. Cut it out (ask for permission first!), and glue it to a piece of drawing or construction paper. Use a cotton swab to dot the paint on the picture. Cover each color in the picture with the same color of paint. To change the shading of the picture, paint white dots to add highlights and black dots to add shadows.

As you dot in the colors, you can mix them together to create new colors. Mix red and yellow dots together for orange areas; mix blue and yellow dots together for green areas. Use dots to add shading and highlights to your picture. You can darken green areas with blue dots or lighten red areas with pink dots. Use your imagination and experiment with different color combinations.

CROSSWORD PUZZLE

24

This crossword puzzle has a surprising twist because your clues are pictures instead of words.

What You'll Need: Graph paper, pencil, tracing paper, black felt-tip pen, markers

Think of words to go in your crossword puzzle, making sure one word can connect with another word. Make your answer key using the graph paper. Draw a square for each letter of each word in your puzzle, connecting the words with a shared letter. Write each letter in. Then number each word going across and each word going down.

Cover the crossword puzzle with tracing paper to copy the squares without the letters in them, or redraw the puzzle without the letters on a new sheet of graph paper. Draw a clue for each word, and number the clues to match the word. If the word for 1 across is dog, then draw a dog for clue 1 across. Draw a decorative border around the puzzle. Make photocopies of the crossword puzzle to give to your friends and family.

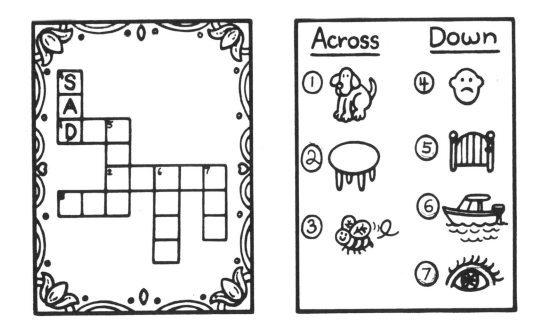

STAINED GLASS PICTURE

25

Create a picture that looks like stained glass. It's just as pretty, and it isn't breakable.

What You'll Need: Construction paper or poster board, pencil, food coloring, small squeeze bottle of white glue, toothpick, crayons or markers

Draw a picture on a piece of construction paper or poster board. After you've drawn the picture, use lines to divide it into "pieces" like a stained glass window. Add 5 to 10 drops of food coloring to the bottle of glue. Squeeze a line of glue along the lines to outline each big shape. Use a toothpick to wipe away excess glue. When the glue dries, color in each area with crayons or markers to give your picture a stained glass look.

BATHTUB ART

26

When you're done with one foamy picture, lightly wipe your hand over the surface and you have a new canvas.

What You'll Need: Shaving cream or nondairy whipped cream, bathtub wall or baking sheet, design tools such as a comb, washcloth, or sponge, food coloring

Here's a fun project to do while you are in the bathtub. Cover a side wall of the tub with a big handful of shaving cream. Use your fingers, a comb, a washcloth, or a sponge to draw a picture in the shaving cream. If you want to make a different picture, wipe your hand over the surface of the shaving cream and start all over again. When you are done creating your bathtub art, make sure you rinse off the shaving cream from the bathtub wall.

If you are not in a bathtub, use a baking sheet as your canvas. Place a handful of shaving cream or nondairy whipped cream on the sheet. Add a drop of food coloring to the cream and blend together. Now you're ready to create some fun art.

BULLETIN BOARD DISPLAY

27

With your very own bulletin board, you always have a place to keep important notes, party invitations, or special photographs.

What You'll Need: Newspaper, corkboard or bulletin board with a flat wood frame, masking tape, acrylic paint, paintbrush, paper towels, blunt scissors, pencil or pen, plastic coffee can lid, sponge

Cover your work surface with newspaper. Place masking tape around the edges of the cork, inside the frame. Paint the frame in a color to match your room. If any paint gets on the cork, wipe it off with a damp paper towel. Let the paint dry.

Cut a small circle from the plastic coffee can lid. To make your stencil, sketch a shape on the plastic circle; make sure it is not wider than the corkboard frame. Cut the shape out. Dip a damp sponge in paint and dab off the excess. Place your stencil on the frame and fill the stencil in by dabbing the sponge straight up and down. Repeat your pattern all around the frame. Let the paint dry.

FOIL PRINTMAKING

28

This printing technique allows you to transfer a picture piece by piece.

What You'll Need: Newspaper, heavy-duty aluminum foil, ballpoint pen, ruler, poster paints, paintbrush, drawing paper, paper towels

Cover your work surface with newspaper. Draw a square on a sheet of foil. Make the square slightly smaller than the paper sheet you will print on. Then draw a picture in the foil square. Select one color of paint, and paint in the parts of the picture using that color. Then place a sheet of paper over the foil print and press. Carefully peel off the paper, and let the paint dry. Use a damp paper towel to wipe off the old color from the foil. Now select a different color, and paint in another area of the picture. Reprint it on the paper as before. Continue reprinting the paper until you use all your colors and your picture is complete.

ORIGAMI LEAP FROG

29

Origami is the Japanese art of folding paper into objects.
Turn a piece of paper into a frog and race it across the table.

What You'll Need: One 3×5-inch blank index card, pencil

1. Follow the illustrations to fold the index card. Fold point A to point D. Unfold and repeat with the other corner, folding point B to point C.

2. Fold the top half of the paper back and then unfold it.

3. Holding the sides at point E and point F, push them in together toward the center.

4. Press the top half of the paper down, creating a triangle.

5. Fold the point G corner of the triangle up to point I at the top of the triangle, and form a small tri-angle. Repeat with the other corner of the large triangle at point H.

6. Fold the tiny triangles in half, lengthwise. Then fold each side of the index card in about ¼ inch.

7. Fold the bottom end of the index card up about ¾ inch. Then fold that piece down in half. Turn your frog over, and draw on eyes. Press your finger on the frog's back to make it leap.

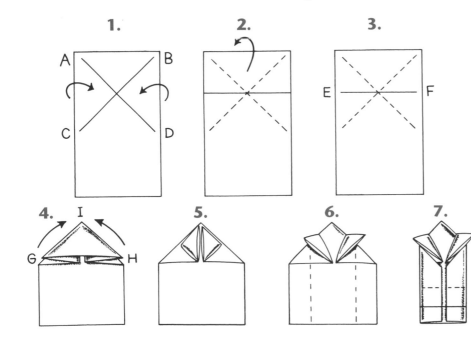

EMBOSSING PAPER

30

This is a double treat since collecting your supplies is as much fun as making the embossed paper itself.

What You'll Need: Lightweight paper, flat objects such as paper clips, keys, or buttons, posterboard (optional)

Look for flat objects, such as paper clips and keys, around your house. Place a piece of lightweight paper over a paper clip and rub over the paper with your finger. Lift the paper, and notice the textured shape on the paper. You've just created embossing paper.

To make embossed designs, rub over an object and move it around under the paper. Use a key to make the petals of a flower. Or cut a wavy edge on a strip of posterboard, and use it to make an embossed line at the top and bottom of your paper. It's a pretty decoration for stationery.

SHADES OF COLOR

31

One color can be quite interesting. Just add a little white or black to create different tones.

What You'll Need: Newspaper, pencil, clean plastic egg carton or small dishes, drawing paper, watercolor or poster paints, paintbrush

Cover your work surface with newspaper. Sketch a picture on a piece of paper. In the empty egg carton, put a small amount of 1 color into 7 different sections. Mix in 1, 2, and 3 drops of white paint with 3 of the sections. Then mix in 1, 2, and 3 drops of black paint with 3 other sections. Do not mix any other colors in the seventh section.

Now paint your picture using the 1 color and the various tones of that color. For example, if your picture is a baseball game and the color you choose is green, then you can paint it in shades of green: dark green stands, light green uniforms, and medium green grass. Think about the direction the sun will shine on the field. Place lighter shades facing the light and darker shades away from the light to make shadows.

FLOWER EXPLOSION

32

If you thought sponges were only for cleaning up messes, you're in for a surprise with this colorful project.

What You'll Need: Construction paper, pencil, blunt scissors, craft glue, heavyweight paper, newspaper, poster paints, paper plates, sponge

Fold a piece of construction paper in half. Draw half of a vase shape at the fold. Cut along the lines of the shape, and unfold the paper. Glue the vase shape on a piece of heavyweight paper.

Cover your work surface with newspaper. Place poster paints on paper plates. Dip a damp sponge in the paint, and then sponge paint "flowers" on the paper above the vase. Twist the sponge to create swirled flowers, or press the sponge on the paper for stamped flowers. You can use this technique to make a bowl of sponged fruit, a tree with sponged leaves, or cornucopia with sponged vegetables.

PERSONAL POSTCARDS

33

Instead of writing a letter, why not send a personal "hello" to your friends and relatives with handmade postcards?

What You'll Need: Cardstock or 4×6-inch blank index cards, ruler, blunt scissors, black felt-tip pen, colored pencils or markers

Cut a 4×6-inch piece of cardstock. On one side of the cardstock, create the back of a postcard. With the ruler, draw a straight line down the center of the card to divide one half for the address and the other half for the greeting. On the half for the address, use a ruler to draw 3 straight horizontal lines from the middle to the bottom of the card. On the other side of the card, create the front of a postcard. Draw yourself at the beach, on a roller coaster, or hiking up a mountain to illustrate your vacation. Your postcard doesn't have to show a real vacation. Draw yourself piloting the space shuttle. Color the picture with colored pencils or markers.

BATIK T-SHIRT

34

The great thing about batik T-shirts is that no matter how many you make, each one will be different.

What You'll Need: Large plastic bag, white T-shirt, fabric marker or pencil, old crayons, paper cupcake liners, disposable paintbrushes, fabric dye, rubber gloves, paper towels, iron and ironing board

1. Cover your work area with a large plastic bag. Lightly draw a design on your T-shirt. Remove the paper wrapping from the crayons. Have an adult melt the crayons in paper cupcake liners in the microwave.

2. Paint the melted crayons on your design. Let it dry. Then crumple up the T-shirt. This is what creates the cracked look of batik.

3. With an adult's help, mix the fabric dye according to package directions. Be sure to wear rubber gloves. Soak the T-shirt in the dye for about 10 to 15 minutes. Cover an area of your work surface with paper towels. Place the T-shirt flat on the paper towels to dry.

4. With an adult's help, iron the T-shirt between 4 layers of paper towels. The paper will soak up the excess wax.

draw

paint

crumble

dye

iron

OPPOSITE ADS

35

Make two or three ads for the same pretend product. Then show them to your friends to see which one "sells" your product the best.

What You'll Need: Drawing paper, colored pencils, markers, or crayons

How would you sell the worst video game, the yuckiest cookies, or the dumbest school? How could you eat, much less sell, computer chip cookies or slimy cookies? Advertisements always have a picture or a photo, writing called copy, and a headline. Invent your own yucky product. Draw a picture and headline for the worst ad, and give your product an awful name. If you don't want to sell something bad, sell something that isn't usually for sale. Sell a field trip, honesty, or a dentist appointment.

SAND CASTING

36

If you take your time and use a little patience, you can create beautiful sculptures to enjoy forever.

What You'll Need: Newspaper, pie pan, brown or white sand, vegetable oil, ruler, tools such as a small spoon, knife, and toothpicks (to make impressions in sand), plaster of paris, paper clips

Cover your work surface with newspaper. Fill the pie pan about half full with sand. Add oil until the sand sticks together. Pat the sand base down to about 1 inch thick in the pie pan. Build up a ½ to ¾-inch rim around the edges. Use a small spoon or knife to press in a design, dig holes, or build ridges in the sand. Use a toothpick to create finer lines or letters. If you are making projections such as legs or stems, place straightened paper clips in the sand to strengthen your plaster casting.

Have an adult help you mix the plaster of paris following package directions. Carefully spoon the plaster into the sand mold. If you'd like to hang your plaster casting, press a paper clip into the top edge. Let the plaster set overnight. When it's dry, remove your cast from the sand and brush off excess sand.

CRAYON & PAINT

37

It's fascinating to see how crayon and paint mix together to make a most unusual texture.

What You'll Need: Newspaper, drawing paper, crayons, watercolor paints, paintbrush

Cover your work surface with newspaper. Draw a beach scene on a piece of paper using crayons. Lightly color in the blue sky, the light brown sand, and the bright beach towels and umbrellas. Now recolor the picture using watercolor paints. Use blue paint over the blue crayon, light brown paint over the light brown crayon, and the same paint colors over the bright beach towels and umbrellas. Let the paint dry.

Now try creating an abstract design. Draw geometric shapes and patterns using crayons. This time, paint over the crayons using different colors. Try to create a mood with your color combinations. (See Emotional Painting on page 55 for mood colors.)

SHIRT PAINTING

38

House paint turns a T-shirt into something cool—especially if you use the colors in your very own home.

What You'll Need: White T-shirt, newspaper, large plastic bag, sponges, blunt scissors, water-based house paint, clean foam food tray (from fruits or vegetables only), scrap paper

When house paint gets on clothes, it won't come off. Here's how you can use it to your advantage. Place your T-shirt over spread-out newspaper. Put a large plastic bag inside the shirt, between the back and front. To paint your shirt, make some printing stamps using sponges. Cut sponges in the shape of a star, crescent moon, and sun. Put some house paint in the foam tray and dip a damp sponge in the paint. Dab off the excess paint on scrap paper. Now print your design on the shirt, covering any existing house-paint stains. Let the paint dry completely.

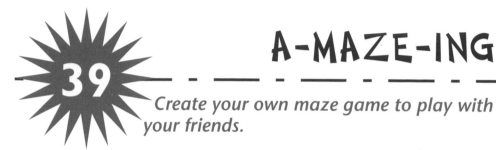

A-MAZE-ING

Create your own maze game to play with your friends.

What You'll Need: Pencil, tracing paper, black felt-tip pen, graph paper, colored pencils

Use a pencil to draw a zigzag track on tracing paper. Add detours and dead ends off the track, and add more tracks that go nowhere. You can also make more maze tracks that are curved or triangular. Once you've completed the maze, go over it with a black felt-tip pen. Then trace over your maze with graph paper so that you won't see any pencil marks. Add a drawing at the entrance and exit such as a lost bear looking for its den. Color the maze with colored pencils. Make copies of your maze game, and give it to your friends to play.

GREASE CASTING

Try a different technique to make plaster casts. This one is so much fun since you can easily "erase" your design and start over.

What You'll Need: Newspaper, blunt scissors, heavy-duty aluminum foil, ruler, shortening, but-ter knife, ballpoint pen, plaster of paris, plastic spoon, paper clip (optional)

Cover your work surface with newspaper. Cut a 4×6-inch square or 6-inch circle from aluminum foil. Fold up the sides about 1 inch. Use a knife to spread a ⅛-inch-thick, even layer of shortening in the foil shape. Press the ballpoint pen into the grease to draw your design. Don't worry if you make a mistake or want to change your design. Just use the knife to smear the grease, and start your design over again.

With an adult's help, mix the plaster of paris according to package directions. Carefully spoon it over the grease. If you'd like to hang your plaster casting, press a paper clip into the top edge. When the plaster is set, pop it out of the foil. Clean the plaster casting with warm, soapy water. Let it dry completely.

BUCKSKIN

▼▼

Explore the history of Native American symbols by re-creating their beauty on pretend pelts.

What You'll Need: Brown grocery bag, blunt scissors, pencil, pastel chalks, hairspray (optional), craft glue or transparent tape

Cut a brown grocery bag in the shape of a pelt. Crumple up the paper until it becomes very soft. Flatten it, then draw a buffalo, sun and moon, or feathers. Color in the picture using pastel chalks. If you want, have an adult spray it with a very light coat of hairspray to set the chalk.

Another idea is to make a ceremonial shield instead of a buckskin. Cut the brown paper bag in a circle instead of a pelt shape. Crumple the paper, then flatten it and draw a Native American design on the paper. Cut out paper strips to create fringe. Glue or tape the paper strips to the paper circle.

PALETTE PAINTING

● ●

This technique uses dabs and dots of paint instead of straight lines, adding dimension to your artwork.

What You'll Need: Cornstarch, poster paints, small containers, craft stick or butter knife, cardboard

In a small container, mix a small amount of cornstarch with poster paint until the mixture becomes thick like pudding. Repeat with other colors of paint. Now "paint" a picture on a piece of cardboard. Use a craft stick or butter knife to apply the thick paint to the cardboard. The paint will "stick up" from your paper. Try an abstract design first. Create "heavy" areas of color by building up the thick paint; to make "light" areas of color, spread the paint out. Then try to "paint" a portrait of someone. Since you are painting with a craft stick, you won't be able to add a lot of detail.

ART IN PIECES

43

One picture is worth 1,000 giggles when you try drawing a picture in nine separate sections.

What You'll Need: Old magazines, ruler, pencil, blunt scissors, drawing paper, craft glue, colored pencils

Find a picture you like in a magazine. Draw a large square around it, then divide it into 9 equal squares. Cut out the small squares. On a piece of drawing paper, draw the picture in 1 cut square; you can even turn the square upside down to concentrate on the lines. As you draw, concentrate on the spacing of the lines rather than the outline. Repeat this drawing technique for each square.

After you're done drawing, cut out the squares, reassemble your picture on a piece of paper, and glue in place. Color in your picture. Another idea is to fill in your square pieces before you put them together using different coloring tools. Color some in with crayon, chalk, and even acrylic or watercolor paints.

CLAY PENCIL HOLDER

44

This unique holder keeps all your pens and pencils close at hand and neatly organized.

What You'll Need: Assorted colors of polymer clay, waxed paper, rolling pin, pen or marker, aluminum foil, butter knife

Roll pancakes of red, orange, yellow, green, blue, and purple clay on waxed paper. Stack them on top of each other in the colors of the rainbow, then cut them into a 1½ × 7-inch rectangle. (This will hold about 8 pencils. If you want it to hold more pencils, than make the rectangle longer.) Bend the rainbow clay into a big arch with your hands. Using a pen cap, poke a hole in the clay about ¾ inch from one end. Make sure it is deep enough to hold a pen or pencil. Make 7 more holes, each about ¾ inch apart. (If you want more pencils in the holder, poke more holes in the longer rectangle.)

With an adult's help, bake the clay arch according to package directions. Wad up some foil and place it under the arch for support. Once the clay has baked, let it cool and then put your pencils in the holder.

STRAW-BLOWN PAINTING

45

Here's a great way to make a splashy picture in wild colors—without even touching the paper!

What You'll Need: Newspaper, removable tape, drawing paper, poster paints, plastic drinking straw

Cover your work surface with newspaper. Tape a piece of drawing paper in the center of your work area. Dilute the poster paint with a little bit of water. Place one color of diluted poster paint on the paper. Now use your straw to blow the paint around on the paper. Before the paint dries, add another color and splash it around. Let the paint overlap and blend. Try blowing your paint from one corner or out from the center. When you're finished painting, let the paint dry.

46

QUILT PICTURE

This looks like an old-fashioned quilt, but there's no sewing and it takes less time than the real thing.

What You'll Need: Pencil, graph paper, ruler, blunt scissors, lightweight cardboard, fabric scraps, craft glue, old paintbrush

Practice drawing your quilt design on a piece of graph paper. Use a ruler to help you draw the triangles and squares of the quilt pattern. Then measure the exact size of the triangles and squares in the design and cut them from cardboard to make the pattern pieces. Place each pattern piece on the fabric scraps and trace around it. Cut out the fabric pieces. Use an old paintbrush to coat the back of each piece with glue. Following the quilt design you drew on graph paper, glue the fabric on the cardboard. After it's dry, trim the cardboard and frame your quilt picture (see Framed Art on page 13).

CORN SYRUP PAINT

47

Corn syrup paint dries with a shiny gloss. It almost looks as if the colors are still wet.

What You'll Need: Newspaper, corn syrup, measuring spoon, food coloring, clean plastic egg carton, heavyweight white paper, black crayon, paintbrush

Cover your work surface with newspaper. To make the paint, mix 1 tablespoon of corn syrup with 5 or 6 drops of food coloring in a section of the empty egg carton. Repeat with the other colors of food coloring, keeping each paint mixture in a separate egg carton section.

Using a black crayon, draw a design with thick outlines on a piece of heavyweight white paper. If you draw a baseball player, outline his pants, shirt, arms, and head with thick black crayon lines. Color in each section with the corn syrup paint; don't let the colors touch one another across the black lines. This homemade paint is also great for drawing a jack-o'-lantern or Christmas tree. Since the paint is so shiny, it will seem like your pictures are all lit up!

POSTER REDESIGN

48

Take an old poster and make it brand new. All you have to do is let your imagination run wild.

What You'll Need: Newspaper, large poster, poster paints, paintbrush, markers, blunt scissors, pencil, construction paper, removable tape

Tired of the same old poster hanging in your room? Make your old poster into a new one. You can make Michael Jordan play football. Cover your work surface with newspaper. Now just paint a football helmet and uniform on Michael Jordan. Let the paint dry and hang your new poster on the wall. Or make a poster of puppies into a poster of the latest space aliens. Use markers to draw in antennas on the puppies, spaceships in space, and stars in the sky.

Use these new posters as a game for your next party. You can play pin the helmet on Michael or pin the antenna on the space alien puppies. Draw helmet or antenna shapes on construction paper. Cut them out, put a piece of removable tape on the back of each, and use them as the game pieces to "pin" on the poster.

FRAMED STAINED GLASS

49

Frame a stained glass work of art, and share its beauty with your family and friends.

What You'll Need: Picture frame, paper towel and glass cleaner, electrician's tape or duct tape, newspaper, black marker, acrylic paints, cornstarch, small containers, squeeze bottle or plastic sandwich bag, blunt scissors, paintbrush

Cover your work surface with newspaper. Have an adult remove a piece of glass from a picture frame. Carefully wipe it with glass cleaner and a paper towel to remove any dust or smudges. With an adult's help, put tape around the edges of the glass. Then draw your design on the glass using black marker. Use lines to break up the picture into shapes with a geometric background.

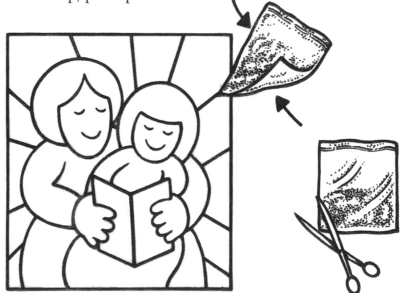

Add in 1 teaspoon of cornstarch at a time with black acrylic paint until it becomes thick like frosting. Put the mixture in a squeeze bottle or in a plastic sandwich bag; cut a tiny piece off the tip of the bag. Carefully squeeze the mixture over your marker outline. Let it dry completely. Thin acrylic paints with water in small containers. Paint in the stained glass design. After the paint has dried, remove the tape and place the glass in the frame.

DECORATE A DOOR

50

Turn your bedroom into a magical wonderland. Decorate the door as the entrance to your favorite place.

What You'll Need: Measuring tape, scissors, butcher, wrapping, or mailing paper, markers or poster paints and paintbrush, removable tape, old magazines, craft glue

Measure your bedroom door. Cut out a rectangle the same dimensions as your door from paper. Cut out a hole for the doorknob. Use markers or poster paints to decorate the paper. You can create an underwater scene, a skiing scene, or a giant "do not disturb" sign. Tape it to your door.

If you don't want to draw or paint a scene, make a giant collage for your door decoration. Cut out pictures from old magazines. Glue them to the paper, covering the whole sheet. After the glue has dried, tape the collage to your door.

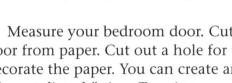

FOIL EMBOSSING

51

Whether you emboss one pretty flower or a wild abstract design, these wall hangings will shine in any room.

What You'll Need: Poster board or cardboard, scissors, craft glue, aluminum foil, markers

Have an adult cut 2 backing pieces of poster board or cardboard into the size of the picture you want to make. It's best to start with a small piece, about 8×10 inches. Cut out some geometric shapes from poster board or cardboard. Glue them in a design on one of the backing pieces. For example, arrange triangle shapes into a pinwheel or square shapes into a checkerboard. Or ask a friend to trace your profile from a shadow. Cut out your profile, and glue it on the backing.

After the glue has dried, place a piece of foil over the top of the shapes and rub until the design is raised onto the foil. Leave the foil in place and color the raised design with permanent markers. Then carefully remove the foil, and glue it on the other backing piece.

LETTER DESIGNS

52

Use your imagination to make your own personalized nameplate for your bedroom door or to create a fun alphabet game.

What You'll Need: Colored pencils or markers, drawing paper, ruler, cardboard, scissors, craft glue, hole punch, yarn

On a piece of drawing paper, draw an object in the shape of its first letter. For example, the word *snake* starts with an *s*. Draw a snake in an s shape, and then write out the rest of the letters. Color in your letter design. Try making a poster of all the letters in the alphabet with letter designs.

To make a nameplate, cut one 3×8-inch rectangle from a piece of paper and one from cardboard. Draw an object in the shape of each letter in your name on the paper. Then color in each letter design. Glue the paper on the cardboard, then punch a hole in the top two corners of the nameplate. String it with a piece of yarn to hang it up on your door.

SALT CLAY DOUGH

53

Do something unexpected. Sculpt sports equipment, such as a bat and ball, or even food, such as pizza and hot dogs.

What You'll Need: 1 cup salt, 4 cups flour, mixing bowl and spoon, 1½ cups warm water, waxed paper, aluminum foil, acrylic paints and paintbrush (optional), resealable plastic bag or airtight container.

Mix salt and flour in a bowl. Slowly begin adding in water until the mixture forms a doughlike consistency. Place a sheet of waxed paper on your work surface, and sprinkle it with some flour. Knead the clay dough until smooth. Sculpt clay into any shape you want, and then bake your sculpture on aluminum foil with an adult's help. Bake thin objects for about 30 minutes at 350 degrees Fahrenheit. Larger or thicker objects will require more baking time. After your clay creations have cooled, add some color with acrylic paints. Let the paint dry. Store unused clay in a resealable plastic bag or airtight container.

PAPIER-MÂCHÉ BANK

54

Save your nickels, dimes, and quarters for a rainy day with a fun-to-make piggy bank.

What You'll Need: Large (6 inch) balloon, small (3 inch) balloon, masking tape, scissors, cardboard, paper towel tube, construction paper, flour and water (for paste), newspaper, 1×4-inch newspaper strips, pencil, pink pipe cleaner, craft glue, pink poster paint, paintbrush

To make the pig's body, blow up the large balloon and tie the end closed. For the pig's head, blow up the small balloon and tie the end closed. Tape the head to the body. Have an adult cut 2 ears from cardboard, cut the paper towel tube in fourths for the legs, and cut and roll a small piece of construction paper for the snout. Tape them to the balloon head and body.

Cover your work surface with newspaper. See the Papier-Mâché Mask on page 17 to make the paste. Dip a strip of newspaper in the paste. Rub the strip between your fingers to remove any extra paste. Put the strip over the balloon body, then smooth in place. Repeat until the body is covered in a layer of strips. Then cover the head, legs, ears, and snout with a layer of strips. Apply 3 or 4 more layers of strips. Let it dry overnight. Wrap a pink pipe cleaner around a pencil to make a tail. Glue the tail on the pig. Then paint the pig with poster paint. Have an adult cut a $\frac{1}{2} \times 1\frac{1}{2}$-inch slot in the top for your coins, and remove and discard the balloon.

55 WILD & CRAZY MONSTERS

In this project, you begin with a good story and make it even better. It's a test for your imagination.

What You'll Need: Drawing paper, pencil, markers

Read a book about imaginary monsters such as *Where the Wild Things Are* and then create your own make-believe creatures. Sketch a fun or scary monster on a piece of paper and color it in. Or use the drawing technique in The Art of Tracing on page 41 to create an outline of a shape, such as a bear. Turn it into a monster by adding horns, sharp teeth, and a tail. Then color it in. Make all kinds of monsters—a giant one, a ghostlike creature, or a dragonlike animal—to create your own picture book.

HALF & HALF PICTURE 56

Picture this—half the design is a photograph and half the design is original artwork. What a surprise!

What You'll Need: Old magazines, blunt scissors, craft glue, drawing paper, pencil, charcoal or colored pencils, removable tape (optional)

Look through an old magazine for a picture of a person's face. Make sure it is somewhat symmetrical (a picture with similar halves). Cut the picture out, then cut it in half down the middle of the face. Glue one half of the picture on a piece of drawing paper; discard the other half. Use a pencil to sketch in the other half of the face. Try to match the facial features. Then color it in with charcoal or colored pencils.

Once you've practiced this drawing technique, try sketching some other symmetrical pictures such as a person's body, a penguin, or a house. Then instead of gluing the magazine picture to the paper, use removable tape to set the cutout half in place. Sketch in the other half of the picture, then remove the original half and sketch in the rest of the picture.

RICE PICTURES

57

Colored rice gives your picture a grainy texture. Experiment with different dyes such as chalk or even spices.

What You'll Need: Pastel chalk or spices such as ground mustard, cinnamon, and paprika, paper plates, cheese grater, uncooked white rice, construction paper, craft glue, old paintbrush

With an adult's help, grate 1 color of chalk onto a paper plate using a cheese grater. Repeat with other colors, keeping them separate. Or place different colors of spices on paper plates. Mix white rice in with each color. Dilute craft glue with water. Use an old paintbrush to paint a picture with the diluted glue. Choosing one color of rice, hold the paper plate like a funnel and pour the colored rice over the glue. Let it set, then pour off the excess rice. Repeat the process with another area of the picture using a different color.

BRAYER SCRAPER

58

This artwork is all your own since you choose the colors, you select the designs, and you even make the painting tools.

What You'll Need: Pencil, cardboard, blunt scissors, newspaper, finger paints, palette, brayer, finger-paint paper

To make painting tools, draw a comb on the cardboard. Cut it out. Make different combs to create different paint patterns. Make a comb with lots of tiny teeth or a few spaced-out teeth.

Cover your work surface with newspaper. Put some finger paint on a flat palette. Roll the brayer in the paint, then roll the inked brayer in stripes on the finger-paint paper. Run the cardboard combs over the wet paint to create a design. Scrape each comb in a square section of paint to make patchwork designs. Let your painting dry flat on the newspaper. Use this painting technique to decorate gift boxes, book covers, and notecards.

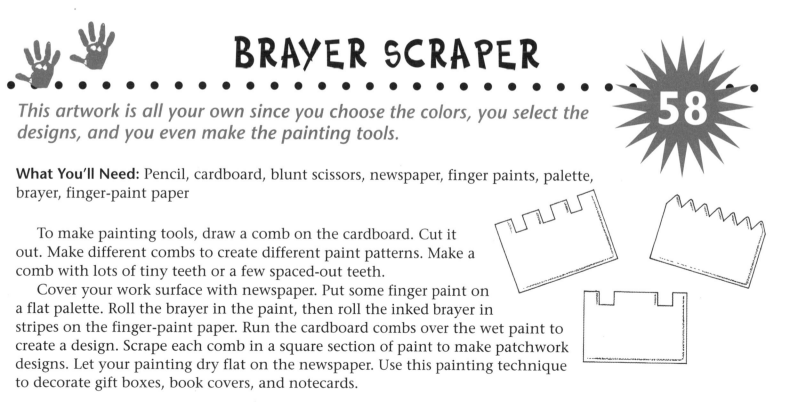

FOAM CORE SCULPTURE

59

Turn ordinary flat cardboard into three-dimensional sculptures. Use your art-work as holiday table decorations or birthday party decorations.

What You'll Need: Markers, 2 foam core boards, craft knife, ruler, trims such as pipe cleaners and pom-poms (optional), craft glue (optional)

Draw the outline of a symmetrical object, such as snowman, on a foam core board. With an adult's help, cut out the shape using a craft knife. Place it on the other foam core board and trace around the shape. Have an adult cut out the second form.

Mark the center of 1 piece, and have an adult cut a slit halfway from the top to the center of the foam. Mark the center of the other piece, and have an adult cut a slit halfway from the bottom to the center. Then connect the 2 pieces by pushing them together through the slits, creating one three-dimensional piece.

Now take apart your sculpture and draw a face on each side. Remember, when you put the 2 pieces back together, half of 1 face should match the half face on the other piece. If you want, decorate your sculpture using all sorts of trims. Glue on pipe cleaners for arms or pom-poms for a nose or buttons.

MARBLE PAINTING

60

You're never boxed in with this unpredictable painting technique. No two designs are ever alike.

What You'll Need: Blunt scissors, drawing paper, removable tape, cardboard box, rubber gloves, poster paints, marbles

Cut a piece of drawing paper to fit the bottom of your box. Tape the paper to the bottom of the box. Wearing rubber gloves, dip a marble in poster paint. Place the marble on the paper. Now tilt, wiggle, and twirl the box around to make designs—the marble is your paintbrush! Let the paint dry. Then use more marbles dipped in other colors to add to your design. Experiment with different colors of paper and paint. Start with red paper and make only white marble tracks. Or try black paper with fluorescent-colored paints. Once all the colors are dry, remove the paper from the box and display your artwork on the wall.

THE ART OF TRACING

61

Tracing an object is just the beginning. The fun comes when you color it in, using imagination and wild designs.

What You'll Need: Old magazines, blunt scissors, lightweight white paper, masking tape, black felt-tip pen, colored pencils or markers

You can trace any picture without tracing paper. Pick a picture from a magazine that you want to trace, and cut it out (ask for permission first!). Tape the picture with a piece of paper over it on a window. You can see the outline of the picture through the paper. Use a black felt-tip pen to trace the outline of the picture. Take the picture and paper off the window. Now add your own details to the outline, and color them in. For example, if you traced a picture of a dog, then draw and color in the eyes, a nose, the fur—or whatever else you want to add. Another idea is to use the shape to make it into something else. Use the outline of a dog to make a monster or space alien instead.

PAPIER-MÂCHÉ MASH

62

This pulpy mash is great for making puppet heads or adding dimension to papier-mâché projects.

What You'll Need: Newspaper, bucket, saucepan, strainer, mixing bowl and spoon, 2 tablespoons craft glue, 2 tablespoons dry wallpaper paste, aluminum foil, paper towel tube, sandpaper, acrylic paints, paintbrush

Tear up 4 sheets of newspaper into stamp-size pieces. Place the newspaper pieces in a bucket and soak them in water overnight. After the paper has soaked, have an adult boil the paper and water in a saucepan for 15 minutes. Stir the paper mixture until it is pulpy. Once the mixture has cooled, use a strainer to press out the excess water. Place the paper mixture in a bowl and add 2 tablespoons of glue and 2 tablespoons of dry wallpaper paste. Stir it well until it thickens. Set the mash aside.

To make a puppet head, create a base form with crushed foil. Wrinkle and crush the foil into the head shape you want. Position the shape over the top of the paper towel tube. Cover the shape with the papier-mâché mash, and sculpt out features. Let it dry overnight. Once it's completely dry, smooth any rough edges with sandpaper, and paint the puppet head with acrylic paints.

SPLATTER PRINTS

63

You're in good shape when you use this terrific painting technique to outline favorite objects.

What You'll Need: Newspaper; old paint shirt; drawing paper; large cardboard box; items to outline such as a pressed flower, leaf, or key; old toothbrush; watercolor or poster paints

Cover your work surface with newspaper. Put on an old paint shirt. Place a piece of drawing paper in the large cardboard box. Place an item such as a pressed flower on the paper. Dip the bristles of an old toothbrush in watercolor or poster paint. Point the toothbrush down at the paper. Now rub your finger over the bristles toward yourself to splatter the paint around the flower. Remove the flower. The splattered paint looks like confetti outlining your picture. Let the paint dry. To create rainbow splatters, use different colors of paints.

THE NEWEST STATE

64

Invent a state that includes all your favorite things—skiing, sailing, amusement park cities, and even towns that sell nothing but ice cream.

What You'll Need: Atlas or map (for ideas), drawing paper, pencil, colored pencils, or markers

In order to add the next state to the union, you need to invent it. Look through an atlas to find a state shape you want to copy. Draw the shape on a piece of paper, and make a map of your new state. Name the state and add geographical features. Draw mountains, lakes, shorelines, cities, and the state capitol. Color in your new state. Then draw the state flag, seal, and flower.

Now create another state. This time make it as silly and illogical as possible. The state motto can be "We live to ski" or "Fast food kingdom." Think of city names to go with the state theme.

PYRAMID PICTURES

65

By overlapping several pieces of construction paper, you're building a picture to create depth.

What You'll Need: Assorted colors of construction paper, blunt scissors, markers, craft glue

Cut a small rectangle from a piece of construction paper. Draw an object or design on it. Cut a slightly larger rectangle from another piece of construction paper using a different color. Glue the small rectangle on top of the larger one. Add more detail to your picture. Then cut an even larger rectangle from another piece of construction paper using a different color. Glue the previous rectangles on top of the bigger rectangle. Draw more designs around your picture. Repeat the process as often as you like to make a pyramid of pictures.

As a variation, you can draw parts of a picture on each piece to create one complete scene. Or instead of rectangles, cut out octagon shapes. Glue them on top of one another, turning them a bit each time to make your picture into a star.

HATCH & CROSSHATCH

66

The art technique uses lines to create highlights and shadows in your drawing instead of coloring it in.

What You'll Need: Drawing paper; pencil, ballpoint pen, or felt-tip pen

The hatch-crosshatch technique uses small lines to create dark areas (shadows) and light areas (highlights) in a drawing. Hatch marks are lines drawn in the same direction, and crosshatch marks are lines crossed over each other in two or three directions. Fewer lines create light areas and more lines create dark areas. Practice this technique to add shadows and highlights to your drawings.

Sketch an outline of a picture, such as an apple, on a piece of drawing paper. Make hatch and crosshatch marks to "color" in the apple. Create shadows along the side and bottom of the apple with crosshatch marks. Highlight the center and the top of the apple with hatch marks.

RIBBON ART

67

Use this weaving technique to create textured artwork that you can hang on the wall.

What You'll Need: Assorted colors of 1-inch-wide satin ribbon (about 3 yards), blunt scissors, ruler, aluminum foil, removable tape, craft glue, water, measuring cups and spoons, small dish, old paintbrush

Cut ribbon into five 9-inch strips. Use remaining ribbon to cut seven 7-inch strips. Cover your work surface with a sheet of aluminum foil. Place the five 9-inch strips on the foil side by side, vertically. Starting 1 inch from the top of the strips, weave a 7-inch strip over and under each ribbon horizontally. Position the 7-inch strip so that 1 inch of each end is left unwoven. Repeat the weaving technique with the remaining 7-inch strips. When you are finished, you should have a 1-inch unwoven border around the edges of the ribbon rectangle. Remove the tape from one side, and weave each end of the ribbon back into a square. Glue in place. Thin about a ¼ cup of craft glue with 1 tablespoon of water. Use an old paintbrush to coat the woven ribbon rectangle on both sides with thinned glue. Let it dry overnight.

TOOTHPICK ARCHITECTURE

68

Create a tiny city, geometric shapes, or a circus tent with clowns. You can build whatever your imagination dreams up.

What You'll Need: Waxed paper, toothpicks, plastic-based clay, poster board

Place a sheet of waxed paper over your work surface. Roll the plastic-based clay into several ¼- to ½-inch balls. (The amount will depend on what you're making since the clay balls are the anchor joints of your toothpick creation.) To make a person, you will need 7 balls of clay; to make a building, you will need 14 balls of clay; and to make a triangle shape, you will need 4 balls of clay. (If you want a permanent structure, use the Modeling Clay Dough on page 16 or the Sculpting Clay Dough on page 12.)

Insert a toothpick into a ball of clay. Connect the toothpick to another ball of clay. Continue connecting toothpicks with the clay until you have completed your structure. Place the finished projects on a piece of poster board to display your architecture.

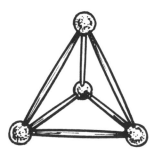

WEAVE A PLATE

69

Jazz up this wall hanging with all sorts of trim—some rough, some smooth, some shiny, and even some unexpected, such as wire.

What You'll Need: Markers, paper plate, pencil, ruler, blunt scissors, yarn, trims such as pony beads or feathers (optional)

Draw a small design in the center of the paper plate with markers. Use a pencil to lightly mark 3-inch increments around the edge of the plate to indicate spacing. Starting about ½ inch from the outer edge of the plate at one of the pencil marks, cut a 2½-inch slit toward the center of the plate. Make sure you don't cut into your center design. Repeat around the whole plate.

Weave pieces of colorful yarn through the slits. Change colors by tying 1 color to another. As you weave the yarn, thread on beads or tie in feathers. When you're done weaving the yarn, knot it in back and cut off excess yarn.

CONTINUOUS PICTURE

70

Here's a drawing challenge. Create a picture using only one line— a long, continuous line.

What You'll Need: Pencil or pen, colored pencils or crayons, drawing paper

Draw a picture on a piece of paper, but don't lift up your pencil or pen as you draw. Make a picture with one long, continuous line. Start drawing a person, then make him or her into a vampire. Start with the mouth, add pointy teeth, and then draw the nose and eyes. Next, fill in the head and body with a bat cape. Just don't pick up your pencil or pen! Try drawing a continuous picture using colored pencils or crayons. Start your drawing in one color, then when you change colors, continue the drawing at the ending point of the last line.

71 SCRATCH BOARD

Etch in a design on scratch board, and you'll see the contrast between dramatic black and bold brights. Your picture practically jumps off the paper.

What You'll Need: Newspaper; card stock or poster board; crayons; black poster paint; dish soap; spoon; bowl; paintbrush; tools such as a metal nail file, toothpick, or pointed craft stick (to scratch in the design)

Cover your work surface with newspaper. Color a piece of card stock or poster board with crayons in assorted colors, covering it completely with a thick layer—color very hard. Mix black poster paint and 2 drops of dish soap together. Paint mixture over the layer of crayon. Let it dry completely. Use a nail file, toothpick, or craft stick to scratch off the paint in a design or a picture, just as if you were drawing a picture on a piece of paper.

2-DAY PAINTINGS 72

This art project uses both your painting and drawing skills. So when it's done, you can show off many talents.

What You'll Need: Newspaper, watercolor paints, paintbrush, watercolor paper, markers

Cover your work surface with newspaper. Use watercolor paints to paint the background of a scene, such as a sunset beach or desert dunes, on watercolor paper. For the sunset beach, paint brown sand, blue water, and an orange-yellow sun setting on the horizon. Blend your colors, and let the paint dry. The next day, draw over the dry painting with markers to create sharp edges and lines. Add the silhouettes of palm trees on the beach or yucca, cactus, and roadrunners to your desert.

You can also create a still life painting using this technique. Try painting a bowl of fruit in washes of color without adding any detail—just use splashes of purple for grapes, red for apples, and yellow for bananas. Wash in a background too. The next day, draw in the shapes of the fruit and the bowl.

BRAYER PRINTING

73

A brayer evenly applies paint to larger areas without brush lines. These are important goals for fine printmaking.

What You'll Need: Brayer, palette (sheet of acrylic or glass), duct tape, newspapers, poster paints, masking tape, finger-paint paper

A brayer, or ink roller, rolls paint evenly and is great for printmaking. To "ink" a brayer, you'll need something smooth and flat to roll the paint on, such as a sheet of acrylic or glass. This will be your palette. With an adult's help, place duct tape around the edges of the palette to cover any rough ends. Before you begin inking, cover your work surface with newspaper.

Place pieces of masking tape across a piece of finger-paint paper to create a stripe design. Put 3 dots of paint on the palette in a row. Roll the brayer in one direction until it is coated with 3 stripes. Roll the inked brayer over the paper to make a stripe design. When the paint is dry, peel off the tape.

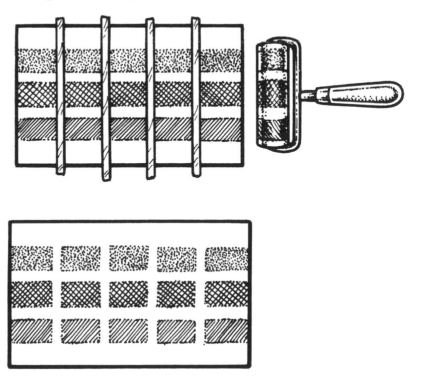

ACRYLIC ON ACRYLIC

74

If you color outside the lines, it really doesn't matter. They're your guide for coloring in a design, and then you erase the lines anyway.

What You'll Need: Scrap paper, ⅛-inch-thick sheet of clear acrylic (available at hobby stores or home centers; cut to fit your desk top), grease pencil, acrylic paints, paintbrush, paper towels

Cover your work surface with scrap paper. Use the grease pencil to draw a design on the sheet of acrylic. Create a theme to match your room, hobbies, or interests. Turn the acrylic sheet over on the paper with the drawing side down. Using the grease pencil outlines as your guide, fill in the design with acrylic paints. Start painting in the middle of the sheet first, then work toward the edges. Let the paint dry. Turn the sheet over and wipe off the grease pencil using a paper towel. Place the acrylic sheet on your desk, paint side down.

FINGER PAINTS #2

75

This is two projects in one. First you finger-paint a design, then you transfer it to another piece of paper.

What You'll Need: Newspaper, 1½ cups liquid starch, ½ cup water, 1 cup flour, small bowls, food coloring, baking sheet or plastic tablecloth, finger-paint paper

Cover your work surface with newspaper. To make the finger paint, mix liquid starch, water, and flour together. Stir until it reaches a smooth consistency. Divide the mixture into several small bowls and add a few drops of food coloring to each bowl. Dip your fingers in the paint and draw your design right on the baking sheet or plastic tablecloth. (Cleanup is easy since this finger paint washes off easily.)

To make a print of your picture, place a piece of finger-paint paper over your artwork and press. Lift the paper off and let it dry flat. Store any extra paint in airtight containers. Place plastic wrap over the surface of the paint to keep the air out.

TESSELLATIONS

76

A tessellation is like a mosaic, using small squares to make a repetitive picture. Try one on your own. It's fun!

What You'll Need: Drawing paper, pencil, ruler, colored pencils

Draw a grid of 9 squares on a piece of drawing paper. On the left side of one square, draw a curvy line. Repeat that same line on the left side of each square. Now draw a different curvy line at the top of the first square. Then draw the curvy line at the top of each remaining square. Take a look at the squares to see what the shape is starting to look like. Fill in more lines to create a shape, repeating the same line in each square. Each line creates part of the next square's design. When you are done, you should have the same shape in each square. Color in your design using colored pencils.

PENCIL PAINTING

Draw a picture, and then turn it into a painting with these "magic" pencils.

What You'll Need: Water-soluble colored pencils (available at art supply stores), drawing paper, paintbrush

Draw a lion on a sheet of drawing paper using yellow and brown water-soluble colored pencils. (They feel and look just like colored pencils.) Then wash over your picture using a damp paintbrush. The colors blend just like watercolor paints. Clean your paintbrush and let the painting dry before you change from blending one color to another color. Add other details.

Water scenes are also fun to paint using these "magic" pencils. Draw a boat at a pier by the lake, using blues for the water. Then use the blending technique to create the boat's reflection in the water. Experiment with other scenes and colors.

POSITIVE-NEGATIVE CUTOUTS

Yes, you'll have lots of fun. No, you'll never run out of ideas. You'll want to do this project again and again.

What You'll Need: Construction paper, ruler, blunt scissors, craft glue

Cut a 4×4-inch square from construction paper. Cut a shape into each side, saving the cutout pieces. Place the cut square and the cutouts on another piece of construction paper. Arrange the cutouts in a mirror image of the square's side shapes. After you've positioned the pieces, glue your design to the construction paper background.

Experiment with all kinds of shapes. You can even glue small cutouts in the center of bigger ones. Or you can tear out the pieces instead of using scissors to cut them. After you've created several cutouts, make them into a collage or frame the finished pieces (see Framed Art on page 13).

STRING ART

79

This project has a three-dimensional feeling. It looks as if the objects you form are actually leaping off the background.

What You'll Need: 8×8-inch square of wood, 29 small nails, hammer, pencil, yarn, blunt scissors, markers

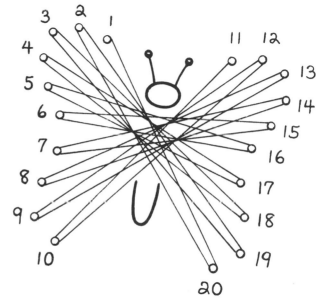

Have an adult hammer the nails into the wood base following the placement shown in the illustrations to make a butterfly and flower. Following the illustrations, pencil in a number next to each nail. This will be your guide when you start to string the design.

To string the butterfly, tie one end of the yarn to nail 1. Then string the yarn from nail 1 to nail 20, then bring the yarn back up to nail 2 and down to nail 19. Continue stringing the yarn using the illustration as your guide. Once you're finished, tie the yarn to nail 11. Trim off excess yarn.

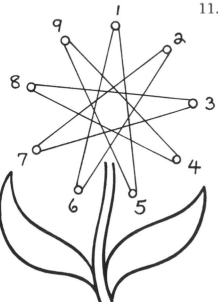

To make the flower, tie one end of the yarn to nail 1. Then string the yarn from nail 1 to nail 5, nail 5 to nail 9, and nail 9 to nail 4. Continue stringing, using the illustration as your guide. When you come back to nail 1, tie yarn to the nail. Trim off excess yarn.

After you've finished stringing, use markers to draw on a stem and leaves for the flower and a head, body, and antennae for the butterfly.

CLAY ACCESSORIES

It's just like having jewelry for your hair when you create this beautiful and very special barrette.

What You'll Need: Blue, white, and yellow polymer clay; rolling pin; waxed paper; craft knife; metal barrette; baking sheet; craft glue; toothpicks (for clay buttons)

Roll out a thin, even pancake of blue clay on waxed paper. Ask an adult to cut clay into a rectangular piece slightly larger than the metal barrette. Knead or roll out a small amount of white and yellow clay. Cut tiny stars and a moon from white and yellow clay. Place them on the blue clay piece.

Bend the clay to match the curve of the barrette. With an adult's help, bake the clay according to package directions. After the clay piece has cooled, glue it to the back of the barrette.

You can also make your own buttons from clay. After you've rolled out the clay, just cut out small circles for buttons. Use toothpicks to punch 2 holes in the middle of each circle, decorate the buttons with other pieces of clay, and bake. After the clay has cooled, sew the buttons on your favorite shirt. (Once baked, the clay buttons can be machine washed and dried on the gentle cycle.)

STATIONERY SET

81

Use these cards to write thank-you letters or to just say "hi" to faraway friends.

What You'll Need: Envelopes, blunt scissors, construction paper, ruled writing paper, craft glue, markers

Use plain envelopes or make your own (see Fancy Envelopes on page 85). To make the notecards, cut and fold over a piece of construction paper, making sure it will fit inside the envelope. Unfold the construction-paper notecard. Cut a piece of writing paper to fit on the notecard, and glue in place. Repeat to make a set of notecards. Use markers to decorate each notecard. Draw a simple design such as a series of stripes, curvy lines, or polka dots. Or cut a rippled edge at the bottom of each notecard so a bit of the writing paper shows. This gives the card a lacelike look. Draw a matching design on the envelopes, leaving room for the postage stamp, mailing address, and your return address.

EMOTIONAL PAINTING

82

Are you feeling blue, green with envy, or pretty in pink? Color a self-portrait to match your mood.

What You'll Need: Newspaper, drawing paper, pencil, watercolor or poster paints, paintbrush

Cover your work surface with newspaper. Draw a picture on a piece of drawing paper. Draw the same picture on another piece of paper, or make a photocopy of your first drawing. Now think of warm and cool colors. Warm colors are the colors of fire: red, orange, and yellow. Cool colors are the colors of ice: blue, green, and purple. Think of what the colors would be for opposite emotions such as love/hate, happiness/sadness, and anger/peace. Once you've assigned colors to the different emotions, paint your pictures. Paint one picture in the colors of one emotion, then paint the other picture in the colors of the opposite emotion. Let the paint dry and compare your paintings.

BUBBLE PRINTS

83

Usually when you blow bubbles, they pop and disappear. Now you can save your bubbles on a piece of paper.

What You'll Need: Baking sheet, plastic cup, plastic drinking straw, ½ cup water, 1 teaspoon dish soap, food coloring, white drawing paper, markers

Mix the water, dish soap, and a few drops of food coloring in a plastic cup. Place the plastic cup on the baking sheet. Place the straw in the cup, and blow bubbles through the straw until they spill all over the baking sheet. Remove the cup and place a piece of paper down over the bubbles. Lift the paper off. The colored bubbles will create a light design on the paper. Let it dry, and then draw in a picture, or outline shapes in the design. Use this bubble-printed paper as wrapping paper, book covers, or stationery.

RESIST PAINTING

84

Here's an idea no one can resist. Use masking paint to block out watercolors and create crisp edges and white spaces.

What You'll Need: Newspaper, white art paper, masking paint (available at art supply stores), watercolor paint, paintbrush

Cover your work surface with newspaper. Draw a picture, such as a candy cane, on a piece of art paper. To paint in the white part of the candy cane, fill it in using the masking paint. The masking paint covers the areas of your painting that you don't want to fill in with color. Let the paint dry. Then paint in the rest of your picture using watercolor paints. Let it dry. Now rub off the masking paint with your fingers. If you want to layer the colors in your picture, repeat the masking and painting process.

Another idea is to paint a soccer player against the blurry background of a stadium. Paint in the player using masking paint; then use watercolor paints to color in the bleachers, the fans, and the grass. When the paint is dry, rub off the masking paint and color in the detail of the player.

REBUS STORY

85

The next time friends come to play, ask everyone to make one rebus story. Then everyone gives their own story to someone else to tell.

What You'll Need: Black felt-tip pen, drawing paper, markers

Create a story with pictures for words. You can make up your own story or use your favorite fairy tale. Write your story on a piece of paper. As you write it down, draw certain words, especially repeated words, as a picture. For example, if you wrote a story about a king, you could draw a picture of a crown as the symbol for the word king. Write and draw a whole story, and bind the pieces of paper together to make a book. (See Mother Moose Illustrated on page 64 for binding instructions.)

You can also make a stamp to repeat the pictures over and over instead of drawing them. See Art Gum Printer on page 69 or Pattern Printer on page 113 to make your own printing stamps.

POLYMER CLAY BEADS

86

Use these four clay beads—rolled stripe, sculpted, impressed, and marbleized—to make beautiful necklaces and bracelets.

What You'll Need: Assorted colors of polymer clay, waxed paper, single-edged razor blade (use with an adult's help), toothpick, jewelry thread, necklace end clasps

rolled stripe

sculpted

Place a sheet of waxed paper on your work surface. Choose the beads you want to make, and follow the instructions below. After forming your beads, carefully insert a toothpick through the clay to create a hole. Then have an adult help you bake the beads following package directions. After the beads have cooled, string them on thread, and then tie on the end clasps to complete your necklace.

Rolled Stripe: Use your hands to roll out 2 thin pancakes, each a different color. Cut 1 rectangle from each. Place one rectangle on top of the other, then roll up tightly. Slice the roll into beads.

Sculpted: Cut a small circle from clay. Cut tiny pieces of different colors, and press them onto the circle to create a design.

Impressed: Cut a small circle from clay. Press a coin into the circle to create an impression.

Marbleized: Roll out 2 colors of clay. Twist them together, and roll into a ball.

impressed

SPONGE PAINTING

87

Use a light technique to sponge paint around your stencils. The result is a perfect background to paint on top of.

What You'll Need: Newspaper, pencil, plastic coffee can lid or plastic plate, cosmetic sponge, assorted colors of stamp pads, drawing paper, colored pencils, crayons, or markers

Cover your work surface with newspaper. Cut out a cloud, snow-flake, or a wave pattern from a plastic coffee can lid. Press a cosmetic sponge on a stamp pad. Place your pattern on a piece of drawing paper and lightly press the inked sponge over the edge of your pattern. Move the pattern around the paper and re-sponge over the edge of it. After you've created your background, let the paint dry. Then draw a scene such as birds in the sky, sleds on the snow, or boats on the sea over the sponge-painted background.

CRAYON SUN CATCHER

88

Melted crayons swirl around to become a kaleidoscope of colors, and the bumpy surface makes a wonderful texture.

What You'll Need: Crayons, handheld pencil sharpener, waxed paper, kitchen or bath towel, iron and ironing board, hot pad or oven mitt, blunt scissors, needle and thread

Twist old crayons in a small handheld pencil sharpener to make shavings. Spread them on a sheet of waxed paper, and place another sheet on top. Cover your "sandwich" with a towel. With an adult's help, iron it until the crayons are melted. Remove the towel, and use a hot pad or oven mitt to smooth over the waxed paper. This will spread the crayons, mixing the colors together. After the crayons have cooled, cut the waxed paper into a flower, a star, or any shape you want. To make a hanger, carefully poke a hole through the top of the sun catcher with a needle. String with thread to hang it in your window.

TIE-DYE T-SHIRT

89

All eyes will be on you when you wear this cool tie-dyed T-shirt with its bright bursts of color.

What You'll Need: White T-shirt, rubber bands, large plastic bag, red, yellow, and blue fabric dye, 3 squeeze bottles, soda ash, scissors

1. To make a bull's-eye design, gather the T-shirt in your hand with the center as one end of the gathered shirt. Tightly wrap a rubber band around the shirt about 2 inches from the center point. Bundle another rubber band about 2 inches down from the first rubber band.

2. Cover your work area with a large plastic bag. Wearing rubber gloves, have an adult help you mix the dye. Pour ½ cup of hot water into each squeeze bottle. Add 1 teaspoon of yellow dye to one bottle, 2 teaspoons of red to another bottle, and 2 teaspoons of blue dye to the third bottle. Add 2 teaspoons of soda ash to each bottle. Screw the lids onto the bottles. Shake well to mix.

3. Place the rubber-banded T-shirt on your work surface. Squeeze the red dye over the first section, squirting into the folds. Apply the yellow dye to the next section, then squeeze the blue dye about 2 inches beyond the last rubber band. Let the shirt set for about 3 hours.

4. After the shirt has dried, rinse each section until the water runs clear. Remove the rubber bands and lay the shirt flat to dry.

3-D PICTURE

90

Outline a simple picture with colorful paper to make it a 3-dimensional work of art.

What You'll Need: Pencil, black and assorted colors of construction paper, blunt scissors, ruler, craft glue, pastel chalks

Draw a car on a piece of black construction paper. Then cut ¾-inch-wide strips from bright-colored construction paper to outline the wheels, doors, and hood of the car. If your car is winding down a country road, outline a tree and a fence. Put a line of glue around the wheels, and stand the paper up in the glue. Bend the paper to match each part of the outline. Outline the whole car in stand-up paper. Use pastel chalks when you are finished to add more color to your picture.

You can also make great ornaments using this technique. After you've outlined your ornament shape, cut it out. Then outline the same design on the other side.

BLOT PAINTING

91

It's like looking in the mirror. Whatever goes on the left side of the paper is reflected on the right.

What You'll Need: Newspaper, construction paper, poster paint, paintbrush, markers

Cover your work surface with newspaper. Fold a piece of construction paper in half, then unfold it. Use a paintbrush to dribble small amounts of poster paint on one half of the paper. Refold the paper, and rub it gently. Unfold it and let it dry. Your picture will have blots of color. To create rainbow-colored blots, mix dots of colors when you dab the paint on the paper. Use markers to draw a design around the blots of color. For example, your blot painting might look like 2 seals balancing 2 balls, so draw in flippers on the seals and stripes on the balls.

SPIN ART

92

This art project will have your head spinning. Watch as paints mix and swirl to become new colors.

What You'll Need: Cardboard box (with high sides), nail, cork or small wood block and hammer, newspaper, blunt scissors, drawing paper or construction paper, removable tape, poster paints, water

With an adult's help, carefully push a nail through the middle of the bottom of the cardboard box so that it pokes through. Then push a cork onto the nail. (Or use a hammer to gently tap a wood block onto the nail.)

Cover your work area with newspaper. Cut a piece of paper to fit inside the box. Tape the paper inside the box to hold it in place. Put dabs of slightly watered-down poster paint all over the paper. Hold the cork (or block) and spin the box. The paint will fly toward the sides of the box. Untape the paper from the box. Place it on your work surface to dry.

PAINT WITH TEXTURE

93

Painting with bumpy paint creates a 3-dimensional effect that will make everyone say, "Wow!"

What You'll Need: Newspaper; textured materials such as sawdust, dry coffee grounds, sand, dried herbs, or washed and crushed eggshells; clean plastic egg carton or small containers; poster paints; pencil; drawing paper; paintbrush

Cover your work surface with newspaper. Place small amounts of textured materials, such as sawdust, in sections of the empty egg carton or in small containers. Add poster paint in each section, and mix the textured materials and paint together.

Draw a picture on a piece of drawing paper. Paint it in with the textured paint. Whether you draw a porcupine or a fire truck, your painting will have a 3-D effect. Use plain poster paint to create smooth areas of paint on your picture.

CLAY PRINTER

94

Print a special message or a unique design with your very own printing blocks to make wrapping paper, notecards, or a wall picture.

What You'll Need: Plastic-based clay, waxed paper, rolling pin, toothpick, craft knife, paper clip, poster paint, pie pan, brayer or paintbrush, drawing paper

Roll out an even pancake of clay about ¼-inch-thick on waxed paper. Have an adult cut it into a 3×5-inch rectangle with a craft knife. Sketch a design on the clay using a toothpick. If you are using letters in your design, write them in backward. (The design will be the raised part of the clay that will print.) Use the knife (have an adult help you) and paper clip to scrape away clay from the design so it is raised.

Place some poster paint in the pie pan, and roll the brayer in the paint. Using the brayer, cover the clay printer piece with paint. If you don't have a brayer, paint the raised part of the clay with a paintbrush. Lay the painted clay over a piece of drawing paper. Press gently to imprint your design on the paper. If you want to use a different color, carefully rinse the paint off the clay printer and repaint it with the brayer to make another print.

MOTHER MOOSE ILLUSTRATED

95

Change the key words of old nursery rhymes or your favorite story to make a silly poem. Then draw pictures to match your new story.

What You'll Need: Drawing paper, blunt scissors, colored pencils or markers, construction paper, hole punch, yarn

Becky had a giant ham. It tastes as bad as liver, and everywhere that Becky went the liver went there with her.

Cut several sheets of drawing paper in half, depending on how many pages you want your book to be. Write a silly story on a page, and draw matching illustrations. For example, instead of Mary having a little lamb, she could have a giant ham. Make yourself, your family, or your friends the characters in the story. Rewrite and illustrate several stories for your Mother Moose storybook. If you want, add a table of contents and dedication page.

After you've finished the inside pages, bind your new book. To make the front and back covers, fold a sheet of construction paper in half and punch 4 holes near the fold. Decorate the front page. Then punch 4 holes in each page, making sure they line up with the holes on the covers. Place the pages inside the covers. Cut a piece of yarn, thread it through the holes, and tie it in a bow.

OPTICAL ILLUSION

96

This project is really a combination of art and magic. When you spin the plate, your design changes in midair.

What You'll Need: Compass, pencil, paper plate, blunt scissors, newspaper, poster paints, paintbrush, hole punch, lightweight string or yarn, ruler

⊠ red
☐ yellow
■ blue

Use a compass to draw a 5-inch-diameter circle on a paper plate, then cut it out. Cover your work surface with newspaper. Paint the primary colors of red, yellow, and blue on the circle, referring to the illustration for placement. Let the paint dry.

Punch 2 holes close together near the center of the circle. Cut a 30-inch piece of string. Thread the string through the 2 holes, and tie it in a loop. Now hold each end of the string loop and rotate your wrists to twist the string. Then pull the strings taut to untwist them, and watch the circle spin. When it spins, the reds, blues, and yellows appear to blend together, creating exciting new colors.

COFFEE FILTER ART

97

With a coffee filter as your canvas, the paint seems to come alive, moving and blending with other colors.

What You'll Need: Newspaper, coffee filters, removable tape, watercolor paints, paintbrush

Cover your work surface with newspaper. Use your hands to flatten out a coffee filter. Tape it flat if necessary. Paint a picture on the coffee filter using watercolor paints. Since coffee filters are made of porous paper, the paint spreads and blends with the colors next to it. Experiment with different abstract designs, then try to make a specific scene. Paint a sun with rainbow rays. Or, since you are working on a round shape, think of painting round pictures such as a sleeping puppy or a baseball mitt. Try painting on other porous papers, too. You can use colored tissue, paper towels, and cotton fabric to create more "blended" pictures.

MARKERS & LINES

98

Draw shapes within shapes and you create an optical illusion. The picture is still there, but it becomes harder to see.

What You'll Need: Drawing paper, pencil, markers

Sketch an outline of a house, yard, tree, and sun. Instead of coloring in the drawing with solid colors, use the markers to "color" it in with lines. Outline each element with marker, and fill the shape in with a continuous line. Or draw concentric shapes within each element until the area is filled in. You can also fill an area with a swirl of lines. If you want to "color in" a sky, draw several smaller areas of shapes and lines to divide it up. Another idea is to write your name and keep outlining it with markers. Use different colors for each outline to create a rainbow progression of colors.

INDIA INK SMOKE

99

Your finished artwork will look like swirled marble. Use the paper to make notecards, book covers, or smoky backgrounds for pictures.

What You'll Need: Newspaper, craft stick or paintbrush, india ink, construction paper, blunt scissors, drawing paper, markers

Cover your work surface with newspaper. Fill a sink or basin with ½ to 1 inch of warm water. Use a craft stick or paintbrush to swirl the water around, and add 2 drops of ink to the water while it's still swirling. Place a sheet of construction paper on top of the water for about 3 seconds. Slowly lift the paper out of the water. The wet paper will curl a bit. Turn it over, ink side up, and lay it flat on newspaper to dry. If you want to make more smoky ink designs, drain the sink and repeat the previous process. Make sure you clean the sink when you're done. To make a note card, cut a sheet of drawing paper smaller than the inked paper. Glue the drawing paper on the blank side of the inked paper; fold the card in half.

SCULPTING CLAY STATUES

100

The only difference between a great sculptor and a really great sculptor is imagination. So let yourself go wild.

What You'll Need: Uncoated wire, waxed paper, rolling pin, white polymer clay (or Sculpting Clay Dough on page 12), aluminum foil, baking sheet, acrylic paints, paintbrush

Have an adult help you with this project. Make a wire shape base for your clay statue. (See the Wire Santa project on page 182 for the bending technique.) Create any shape you want—a person, animal, or even common objects. Artist Claes Oldenburg copied common household objects such as a can opener for his statues.

Cover your work surface with waxed paper. Roll clay into a thin pancake. Place pieces of clay over the wire shape, covering it completely. Use your fingers to smooth over any gaps. Add dimension to your statue by pinching patches of clay over one another or cutting away small areas of clay.

Place your sculpture on a foil-covered baking sheet. To support the shape, crumple some foil pieces and place where needed. Bake the clay statue. (If you are using the Sculpting Clay Dough on page 12, do not bake; let it air dry.) After it has cooled, paint it with acrylic paints.

CRAFT ACTIVITIES

This chapter features craft projects using cut and paste materials, a nature theme, and recyclables. Almost every project calls for scissors. Make sure you use blunt scissors, and always handle and carry them safely. Ask an adult for help with the hard-to-cut items. As you try more projects, you'll learn how to use various tools while experimenting with different ideas. A simple project such as paper lanterns can be adapted in size, color, folding technique, and display. You create the additions that make your project unique. Remember, creativity doesn't always mean making something new, it's learning how to combine one idea with another.

BUTTONS & BROOCHES

101

Recycle your favorite magazines or greeting cards by turning them into custom jewelry—it's as easy as cut, paste, and wear.

What You'll Need: Old magazines or greeting cards, thin cardboard, pencil, blunt scissors, craft glue, trims such as feathers, ribbon, glitter, and sequins, pin back (available at craft stores) or masking tape and a safety pin

Cut a picture from your favorite magazine or greeting card. Place it on a piece of cardboard and trace around it. Cut out the picture shape from cardboard. This will be your back piece. Glue the picture to the cardboard back piece. Let the glue set. Glue on trims, such as feathers, sequins, ribbon, or glitter, to decorate your brooch. Glue the pin back to the back of the brooch, or tape a safety pin on the back. Make more pins to give to your friends, and wear them on button day at school.

ART GUM PRINTER

Make your own rubber stamp from an art gum eraser. Use it to create different geometric patterns on everything from stationery to gift boxes.

What You'll Need: Pencil, art gum eraser, craft knife, stamp pad, drawing paper

Lightly draw a simple design on one side of an art gum eraser. To make the raised part of your design, have an adult help you use a craft knife to carve out the parts you don't want to print. Press the carved side of the eraser down on a stamp pad. Position the eraser on a piece of paper and press down firmly to print

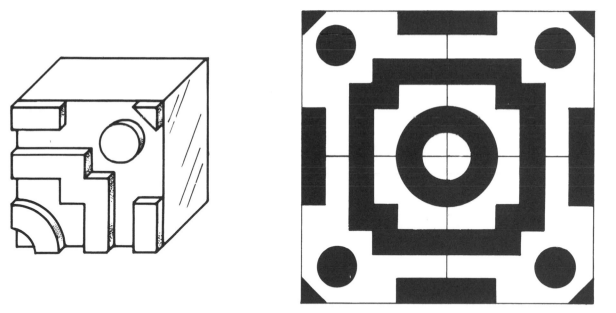

your design. Stamp it in repeated patterns, reinking it every 1 or 2 prints. Be sure to wash the printer when you change colors and when you're done using it.

Make your eraser into a personal stamp for yourself. Instead of carving out a geometric design, carve out your initials on the eraser. Then use the printer to sign important papers with your "mark."

SPIRAL MOBILE

103

Hang your mobile in front of an open window and let the wind gently twirl and whirl your spiral.

What You'll Need: Pencil, 39-ounce-size plastic coffee can lid, scissors, permanent markers or acrylic paints and paintbrush, hole punch, string, mobile items such as shells, acorns, or beads

To make the spiral mobile hanger, draw a 1-inch-wide spiral line on a large coffee can lid. (See illustration for reference.) With an adult's help, cut along the spiral line. Decorate the spiral mobile hanger with acrylic paints or permanent markers. Let it dry.

Punch holes in the mobile hanger along the spiral, making sure the holes line up together on separate parts of the spiral. Punch a hole at the top end of the spiral, and thread it with string to hang the mobile. Pull the spiral hanger open. Tie a piece of string through 1 top hole of the spiral, and string it through 1 hole on each adjacent part of the spiral. Leave the end of the string hanging. This is where you will hang your mobile items. Repeat for remaining holes. Hang shells, acorns, or beads from each string end.

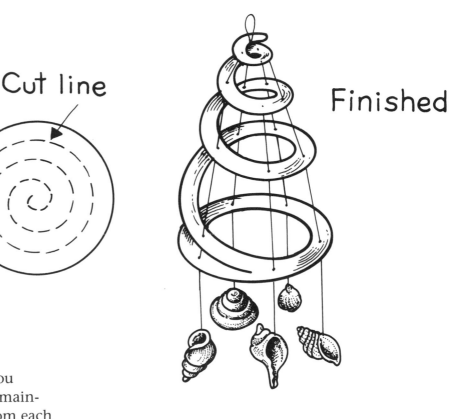

Cut line

Finished

PERSONALIZE YOUR HATS

104

Turn an old baseball cap into a new, stylish hat of your own. The possibilities are endless.

What You'll Need: Old baseball hat or painter's cap (available at paint supply stores), scrap of fabric, scissors, craft glue, fabric paints, paintbrush, markers, glitter, sequins

Have an adult cut a circle or square from a scrap of fabric large enough to cover the front emblem of a baseball hat. Glue the fabric over the emblem. Decorate your hat with fabric paints and markers. Make your baseball hat into a fun beach cap. Paint an underwater ocean scene with fish and seaweed. Use the markers to add detail to the picture. Let the paint dry. Glue on glitter and sequins to make the fish sparkle.

CARD CUTUPS

105

Save your birthday or holiday cards to make card cutups. Use them to create a memory collage, new greeting cards, or special decorations.

What You'll Need: Old greeting cards, blunt scissors, glue, construction paper, markers

Remember your birthday with a memory collage. Cut out the cover designs and inside greetings from old birthday cards. Glue them in a random pattern on a piece of construction paper. Write the date of your birthday on the collage.

To make new greeting cards, fold a piece of construction paper in half. Cut pictures from old greeting cards. Glue them to the front of the construction paper. Then write your own greeting inside.

To make a holiday decoration, cut different pictures from several holiday cards. For example, cut a picture of Santa Claus from one card, a picture of presents from another card, and a tree from a third card. Then glue them together on a piece of paper to make a picture of Santa putting presents under the tree.

CHARACTER COLLAGE

106

Create a family of silly characters with some old magazines, scissors, glue, and your imagination.

What You'll Need: Old clothing catalogs or magazines, blunt scissors, craft glue, construction paper

Look through old clothing catalogs or magazines. Cut out different heads, hairdos, arms, hands, bodies, clothes, legs, and shoes. Now paste the different parts together on a piece of construction paper to make a mixed-up, new character. Be creative—paste a great big hat on a small head and tiny arms on a big body. Make a whole family of characters and give them a silly family name. You can even paste together parts of objects to make an alien character. For example, the alien could have a car-tire head, gift-box body, feather arms, and key legs.

CONFETTI PICTURE

107

This project is like pointillism except instead of painting the dots, you're using colored paper dots to create your picture.

What You'll Need: Hole punch, assorted colors of construction paper, small dishes or containers (optional), pencil, craft glue, heavyweight paper

Punch out dots from different colors of construction paper to make confetti dots. If you want, keep the colors separate in small dishes or containers. Draw a picture, such as a bouquet of flowers, on a piece of paper. Fill in a section of the picture with glue, and sprinkle one color of confetti dots over the glue. Let the glue dry, then shake the paper to remove the excess dots. Continue coloring your picture with more dots. If you want to be more precise, glue single dots in place, one by one, to "paint" your picture.

BALLOON ROCKETS

108

Your balloon engine takes your homemade rocket to new and exciting places. Just hold the end, aim, let it go, and watch it fly.

What You'll Need: Markers, lightweight paper, transparent tape, blunt scissors, ruler, pencil (long, thin) balloons

1. Draw a design for your rocket on a piece of paper. With the design side facing out, bring the ends of the paper together to form a tube. Overlap the ends until the diameter of the tube is slightly larger than the diameter of a blown-up balloon. Tape the ends to secure it.

2. Cut a piece of paper in half, horizontally. Using one half, bring the top ends together and overlap them to form a cone. Tape the ends to secure it. Trim the excess paper at the bottom of the cone. Tape the cone to the top of the rocket. Use the other half of the paper to make the rocket fins. Cut the paper in half, vertically. Cut a triangle from each half. Fold the long side of one triangle in about ¼ inch. Tape it to one side of the rocket. Repeat with the other triangle.

3. Blow up a pencil balloon. Do not tie the end in a knot. Hold the end closed, and place it inside the rocket tube. Let go of the end, and send your rocket to the moon. (Be sure to throw away any discarded balloons when you're finished—they are a choking hazard. And please don't shoot your rocket into anyone's face.)

Form a tube.

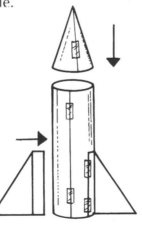

Add a nose cone and fins.

Send your rocket to the moon.

POM-POMS

109

Make a pom-pom in your school colors. Bring it along to the next game and cheer on your team.

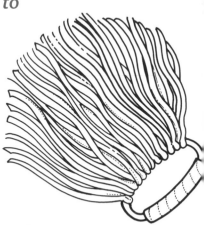

What You'll Need: Plastic bags such as white kitchen bags, clear dry-cleaning bags, black trash bags, or colored shopping bags, tape measure, blunt scissors, heavyweight cotton cord, masking tape

Collect 2 different colors of plastic bags. Cut along each side of the bags. Then cut the bags into 24-inch strips, about 1 inch wide. (The more strips you cut, the fluffier your pom-pom will be.) Hold several strips together and tie them to a long piece of cord. Repeat until you have used all the strips. Slide the knotted strips together on the cord so that they are bunched up next to each other. To make the pom-pom handle, tie the ends of the cord together. Wrap the cord handle with masking tape.

RUBBER BAND ZITHER

110

Bet you didn't think you could make music from a box. Play high and low notes with this homemade instrument.

What You'll Need: Shoe box with lid, scissors, corrugated cardboard, craft glue, rubber bands, markers

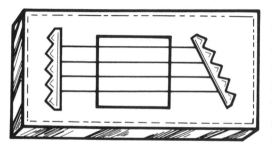

With an adult's help, cut a 4-inch-square hole in the lid of a shoe box. Cut two 1×4½-inch pieces from the corrugated cardboard. Cut a zigzag edge on each piece, creating cardboard "combs." Glue one "comb" to one side of the square hole, and glue the other "comb" slightly angled from the square on the other side. Let the glue set overnight. Decorate the shoe box with markers. Stretch rubber bands from the teeth of one comb to the teeth of the other comb on the shoe box lid. Put the lid on the box. Pluck the rubber bands to play your zither.

TEAR-IT-UP MOSAIC

Take apart a picture to find the basic shapes that make it up, and create an interesting final picture.

What You'll Need: Old magazine, craft glue, water, small dish, old paintbrush, construction paper

Find a picture you like in an old magazine and tear it out. "Take apart" the picture by tearing it up into separate pieces. Look at the major shapes or colors in the picture and tear these pieces out. For example, if your picture has a large area of a color, tear that area into tiny pieces and the rest of the picture into bigger pieces. After you're done "taking apart" your picture, dilute some glue with water in a small dish. Apply the diluted glue to the back of the torn pieces, and glue the pieces of the picture back together on a piece of construction paper. Leave some space between the pieces. This makes your picture look like a mosaic. Let the glue dry.

TERRARIUM

Bring a bit of the outdoors indoors with a terrarium. Add some plants and some plastic animals to make a prehistoric forest in your room.

What You'll Need: Fish bowl, gravel or small pebbles, sand, potting soil, spoon, house plants, aquarium rocks, plastic animals (optional), plastic wrap

Place a layer of gravel or pebbles in the bottom of the fish bowl. Then add a layer of sand. Spread a 2- to 3-inch layer of potting soil over the sand. Use a spoon to dig shallow holes for the plants. Place the plants in the holes to create a miniature forest scene. Sprinkle some aquarium rocks over the soil. Add little plastic dinosaurs or jungle animals to roam through your rain forest. Water the plants lightly. Place the terrarium near a window, keeping it away from direct sunlight. Place a piece of plastic wrap over the top of the fish bowl to keep the moisture in.

BIG BOX BONANZA

113

Turn an ordinary box into something special. With a little imagination, you can make it into a pretty house or a favorite store.

What You'll Need: Big appliance box, scissors or craft knife, newspaper, poster paints, paintbrush, large piece of fabric (optional)

Make your box into a house or store. Have an adult help you cut out windows, shutters, and a door. Then cover your work area with newspaper. Paint flowers, bricks, shingles, or a store sign on the box. Add any trims you want to decorate your house or store. Let the paint dry.

You can also make a puppet stage for the puppet projects in Chapter 3. Cut a big opening in one side of the box. Hang a piece of fabric over the opening to make a curtain. Decorate your puppet stage box using poster paints.

SPOOL-A-WORD

114

Spin the spools to make real or pretend words. Even better, spin letters with your friends and invent new word games.

What You'll Need: Empty wood or plastic spools, permanent markers, unsharpened pencils

Find 3 spools and 1 unsharpened pencil. Using a blue marker, write the letters *s, r, l, g,* and *f* around the first spool. Around the second spool, write the letters *a, e, i, o,* and *u* in red. Around the third spool, write the letters *n, t, d, p,* and *b* in blue. Put the spools on a pencil (in order) and turn them to form a word. Make other spools with more letters, and pick spools with your friends. Put them on a pencil and see who can come up with the most words in one minute.

115 PASTA LACE ORNAMENTS

These decorations not only make exquisite Christmas tree ornaments, but they also look very pretty hanging in a window.

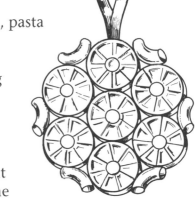

What You'll Need: Waxed paper, water, food coloring, small bowls, mixing spoon, pasta wheels, elbow macaroni, craft glue, ribbon

Cover your work surface with waxed paper. Mix some water and food coloring together in a small bowl. Repeat for other colors. Dip 7 pasta wheels and 6 elbow macaroni pieces in the bowls, alternating colors. Let all pasta pieces dry.

Arrange 6 pasta wheels in a circular pattern with 1 pasta wheel in the center. Apply glue to the sides of the pasta wheels and glue them together. Glue the 6 elbow macaroni pieces around the circle of pasta wheels. To make the ornament hanger, bring the ends of a small piece of ribbon together to form a loop. Glue the ends to the back of the ornament.

DECOUPAGE ART BOX 116

Decorate a plain box using fun cutouts. Find pictures of your favorite things, or look for a theme such as dinosaurs, angels, or flowers.

What You'll Need: Newspaper, blunt scissors, wrapping paper or old magazines (for cutouts), craft glue, water, bowl, old paintbrushes, wooden box (available at craft stores), water-based polyurethane

Cover your work surface with newspaper. Carefully cut out the pictures that you want to paste on your box. Once you have gathered all the pictures you will need to decorate your box, position them on the box to create a scene. Dilute some glue with water. Remove the pictures from the box, and coat the back of the pictures with the diluted glue completely and evenly. Press them back onto the box. Smooth out any bubbles. Let it dry. Apply a coat of polyurethane to the box. Let it dry completely, then apply a second coat.

117 ADVANCED PAPER FOLDING

Learn how to use "scoring" to create fancy paper-folding projects. This technique turns a flat piece of paper into three-dimensional art.

What You'll Need: Heavyweight paper or index cards; scoring guides such as a ruler, compass, or French curve ruler; blunt scissors; transparent tape

Scoring creates an impression on paper to use as a folding guide. This makes it easier to fold the paper into straight, curved, or wavy lines. To score a piece of paper, use a ruler to guide the point of your scissors as you "draw a line" on the paper. To make curvy or wavy lines, use a compass or French curve ruler. Here are some paper-folding ideas to get you started.

Cut out a big circle from a piece of paper. Use a compass to score 2 circles inside it. Cut a slit from the outer edge into the center. Fold 1 inside circle, pinching it along the score line. Turn the paper circle over, and fold the other inside circle. Overlap the cut ends, and tape them together to secure.

Cut out a curved shape from a piece of paper. Use a compass to score 4 curved lines on the shape. Then fold each line, turning the paper over after each fold to alternate the fold direction.

Score some straight lines on a piece of paper. Fanfold the paper along the score lines, then fold in the corners. Open the fanfold, and pinch the top and bottom triangle folds in the opposite direction of each fanfold crease.

ALPHABET ART

118

Spell out the objects in your picture with pasta letters. This art form is called word graphs and it's F-U-N.

What You'll Need: Alphabet pasta, craft glue, drawing or construction paper, markers

Word graphs use words to draw an outline of an object. For example, the words *sun* and *shine* form a sun's shape. The word *sun* is used to outline the round part of the sun, and the word *shine* is used to outline the sun's rays. Gather letters from alphabet pasta to make your picture with words. If you don't have any alphabet pasta, you can still make a word graph—just draw the letters. Glue the alphabet pasta to a piece of paper to make your picture. Fill in any missing letters or add more details with markers.

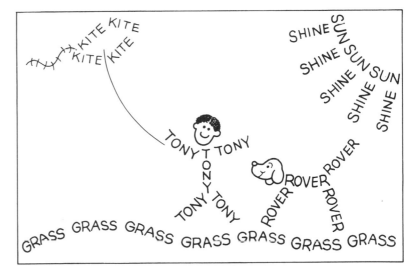

QUILT-PATTERNED COLLAGE

119

Use quilt shapes such as squares, triangles, and hexagons to piece together a patterned collage.

What You'll Need: Old magazines, blunt scissors, ruler, craft glue, construction paper

Make a quilt-patterned collage using magazine pictures instead of fabric. Look for a magazine picture in colors that you like. Once you have selected a picture, cut it into several 2×2-inch squares. Then cut some of the squares in half, diagonally, to form triangles. Now piece your quilt collage together on a piece of construction paper. Once you have arranged the pieces in a pattern you like, glue them in place.

PERSONAL PLACE MATS

120

It doesn't even matter if you get these place mats dirty because they wipe clean with a damp sponge. Now that's neat.

What You'll Need: Markers, 12×18-inch piece of poster board, blunt scissors, cutouts from construction paper or old magazines, craft glue, grease pencil (optional)

Use markers to draw a background, such as a beach, on the poster board. Cut out shapes or pictures from construction paper or old magazines. If you have a beach scene for your background, cut out boats and people. Glue the cutouts on the poster board. Have an adult take you to a copy center store to have your place mat laminated. Leave a ¼-inch plastic border around the place mat.

You can also glue on fun things you want to study, such as maps, sports facts, or poems. Another idea is to draw a maze on your place mat. Once laminated, use a grease pencil and play the game again and again.

MULTICOLORED CRAYONS

121

Don't throw away your old crayons. Recycle them into new multicolored crayons, and draw pictures that change colors with each stroke.

What You'll Need: Old crayons, microwave-safe container, paper cupcake liners

Peel off the wrappers from old crayons. Break up the crayons into ½-inch pieces. Put the pieces into a microwave-safe container. With an adult's help, melt the crayons in the microwave on a high setting for 3 to 4 minutes. Watch the crayons until most of them are melted. Have an adult help you pour the melted crayons in a double-layered paper cupcake liner. Be very careful—the crayon wax will be very hot. Let the wax cool. (You can put it in the freezer for a few minutes.) Pop the new crayon out of the liner to make great multicolored art. This crayon works great with the Rubbings project on page 15.

TOOTHPICK DOLLS

122

These tiny people can keep you company wherever you go.
Slip them into your pocket, notebook, or schoolbag.

What You'll Need: 5 toothpicks, ruler, blunt scissors, embroidery floss, craft glue

1. With an adult's help, cut off 1¼ inches from one end of 1 toothpick. This is the body. For the legs, cut off ⅝ inch from one end of 2 toothpicks. To make the arms, cut off 1¾ inches from one end of the remaining 2 toothpicks. Throw away toothpick scraps.

Wrap floss around toothpicks.

2. Glue 1 leg to each side of the toothpick body. Let the glue set. Apply a dot of glue to the side of 1 leg near the top, and place one end of the embroidery floss on the glue. Wrap the floss around the toothpicks, working your way down. Continue wrapping until you reach ½ inch from the end of the legs. Trim the floss, and glue the end in back.

3. Wrap each toothpick arm with floss. Glue the arms to the wrapped body. To make the shoulders, add a dot of glue to the toothpick body just above the floss. Place the end of the floss on the glue, and wrap it down around the body and the tops of the arms about 6 or 7 times. Trim the floss. Glue the end in back.

Glue arms to the toothpicks.

4. Make the head by wrapping floss into a ball around the top of the toothpick body. Trim the floss, and glue the end in back. To make the hair, cut several strands of floss. Hold the strands together, and glue them to the top of the doll's head. Trim excess floss.

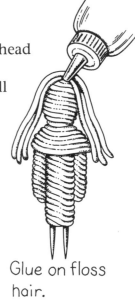

Glue on floss hair.

CUSTOM PILLOWCASE

123

Stencil on your own custom border to turn a plain pillowcase into something special for your room.

What You'll Need: Pencil, plastic coffee can lids, scissors, plain pillowcase, plastic garbage bag, binder clips, acrylic paints, paper plates, stencil brush

Draw a flower shape on 1 plastic coffee can lid. Draw leaf shapes on another coffee can lid. Have an adult cut the shapes out to create a flower stencil and a leaf stencil. Put the plain pillowcase flat on your work surface, and place a plastic garbage bag inside the pillowcase. Place the flower stencil on the edge of the pillowcase, and secure it with a binder clip. Pour some acrylic paint on a paper plate. Dip a stencil brush in the paint, and dab off the excess paint on a piece of paper. Dab the brush inside the stencil

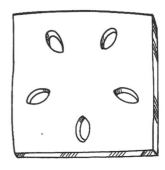

shape until it is filled in. Continue stenciling the flower design along the edge of the pillowcase to make a border. Once the paint has dried, repeat the stenciling process using the leaf stencil and a different color paint. Let the paint dry. If you want, stencil the same border on your bed's dust ruffle or curtains to match your bedroom.

124 JIGSAW PUZZLE

Nothing to do on a rainy day? Make this colorful jigsaw puzzle for hours of fun.

What You'll Need: Poster board, pencil, markers or a magazine picture and craft glue, blunt scissors

Draw a picture on a piece of poster board and color it in with markers. If you don't want to draw a picture, cut out a picture from a magazine and glue it on the poster board. Divide the picture into puzzle pieces. Turn the poster board over and use the pencil to draw separate puzzle sections. The bigger the section, the easier your puzzle will be. Add knobs to each piece at the spot where the puzzle pieces will interlock. (See illustration for reference.) Cut out the puzzle pieces. Now put your puzzle back together again.

PAPER CUTOUTS #1 125

Begin with a flat shape, add a few simple cutouts, and now you have a three-dimensional picture.

What You'll Need: Poster board, pencil or black felt-tip pen, blunt scissors, construction paper, craft glue

Draw an animal shape on a piece of poster board. Cut out the animal shape. Now make its "coat" using paper cutouts. To make fish scales, cut out small semicircles from construction paper. Glue the straight edge of the semicircles to the poster board animal shape, and bend the other ends of the semicircle up to create a three-dimensional look. To make bird feathers, cut out small triangles, glue them to the poster board, and bend them up. For alligator teeth, cut a zigzag line, score each side, glue them to the poster board, and bend the teeth up. To make a curly animal coat, cut out small rectangular strips. Wrap each strip around a pencil to curl it. Glue the curled strips to the poster board.

GLITTER JARS

126

Gently shake your glitter jar. Watch what's inside as it swims and floats back to the bottom.

What You'll Need: White corn syrup, water, small glass jar with a tight fitting lid, food coloring (optional), decorative items such as glitter and sequins, epoxy or super-hold glue, acrylic paints and paintbrush (optional)

Mix corn syrup and water together in the jar. For each 4 ounces of corn syrup, mix in 1 tablespoon of water. If you want to add color to the mixture, put in 1 drop of food coloring. Then add glitter and sequins. You can also add plastic charms such as a little fish to make your jar into an underwater scene. With an adult's help, glue the lid on the jar. Let the glue dry. Decorate the lid and jar using acrylic paints.

HERB COLLAGE

127

See how many different colors, textures, and smells you can find in Mom's spice cupboard to make a scented design.

What You'll Need: Construction paper, craft glue, herbs and spices such as parsley flakes, cinnamon, or chili powder

Make an herbal design on a piece of construction paper. Spread one area of the construction paper with a layer of glue. Cover it with spices such as parsley flakes, cinnamon, and chili powder. Let the glue dry, then shake off the excess spices. Add dots and lines of glue to the design, and sprinkle on more herbs and spices. Once the glue dries, shake off the excess herbs. Experiment with other spices and herbs to add a variety of colors and fragrances to your pictures.

FANCY ENVELOPES

128

Make your own special envelopes to send letters or artwork to your friends and family.

What You'll Need: 9×12-inch piece of cardboard, ruler, pencil, blunt scissors, 9×12-inch piece of medium-weight paper, craft glue

Draw the envelope pattern shown here on a piece of cardboard. Cut out the pattern. Trace the pattern on a piece of medium-weight paper. Cut out the envelope pattern and fold it along the lines indicated on the illustration. Glue all edges except for the top flap. Place your letter or picture in the envelope and seal the top flap. Now you're ready to send your letter.

You can make fancy envelopes using a magazine picture or your own artwork—just make sure it's at least 9×12 inches. Trace the envelope pattern on the back side of the magazine picture or your artwork. Fold and glue your fancy envelope as described above. Stick on 2 white mailing labels for the return and the sender addresses, and it's ready to go. Once you get the hang of this, you can design your own pattern for specialty envelopes of a different size.

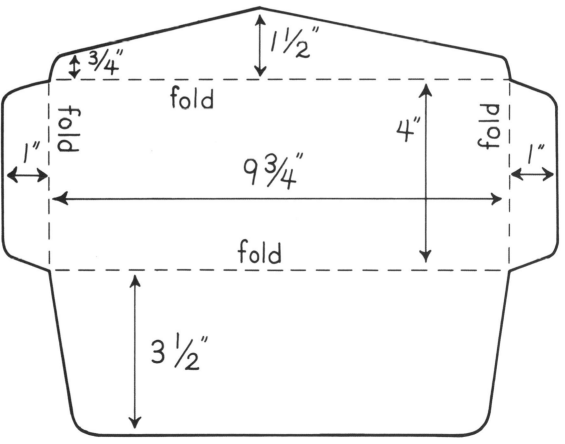

PAPER SNOWFLAKES

129

Place these decorative snowflakes in the window or hang them from a mobile and watch them float in the air.

What You'll Need: White paper, compass, pencil, blunt scissors

Use a compass to draw a 4-inch circle on a piece of paper. Cut out the circle to make a snowflake. To make a 4-point snowflake, fold the circle in half. Then fold it in half again. If you want to make an 8-point snowflake, fold it in half yet again. To make a 6-point snowflake, fold the paper circle in half, then in thirds, and then in half again. Now use the scissors to snip little bits from the paper. Cut into both sides, the top, and the point. Open the piece of paper to see your snowflake.

To add different designs to your snowflake, make more cuts with special tools such as a hole punch or pinking shears. Try using special paper for your snowflakes, too. Make snowflakes with colored foils, magazine pictures, tissue paper, or wrapping paper. Use your snowflakes to hang on the Spiral Mobile on page 70.

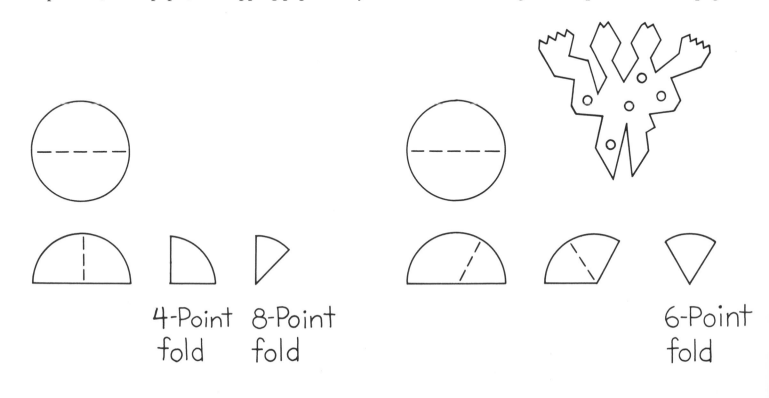

4-Point fold 8-Point fold

6-Point fold

YARN COLLAGE

130

The yarn gives your picture a furry, three-dimensional appearance. Stringing beads on the yarn adds even greater depth.

What You'll Need: Pencil, drawing or construction paper, craft glue, assorted colors of yarn, blunt scissors, beads (optional)

Draw a picture, such as a plane in the sky, on a piece of drawing or construction paper. Apply a line of glue along the outline of the picture. Then place yarn along the glue. To "color in" a space, coil the yarn around itself until the space is filled in. Keep outlining and filling all the spaces in your picture with yarn. Trim off any excess yarn. To add more dimension to the picture, string a few beads on the yarn as you go along.

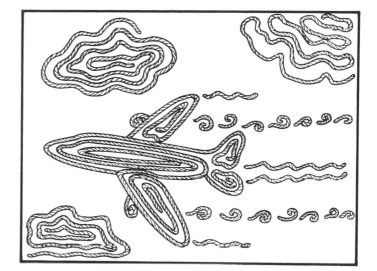

STENCIL ART

131

Believe it or not, you can create geometric-patterned artwork with stencils made from old coffee can lids.

What You'll Need: Plastic coffee can lids, pencil, scissors, drawing paper, colored pencils

Draw a geometric shape—a triangle, octagon, square, rectangle, and circle—on several plastic coffee can lids. Have an adult cut out each shape from the lids. The lid with the cutout shape is your stencil. Place the stencil on paper, and outline or fill in the shape with colored pencils. Use the stencils to color in geometric patterns on paper to make gift wrapping. You can also use the stencils to make geometric pictures such as a round clown with a triangular hat and square hands and feet.

BERRY BASKET WEAVING

132

This is a great basket to hold your treasures. Fill it with dried flowers or candy treats and it makes a great gift, too.

What You'll Need: Plastic berry basket, fabric or ribbon, blunt scissors, construction paper, stapler and staples, tissue paper, goodies

Cut several strips of fabric or ribbon as wide as the openings in your basket. Weave the strips in and out of the slots around the basket. Tie each strip in a knot and trim the excess. To make the handle, cut a 1-inch-wide strip of construction paper. Secure one end of the strip to each side of the basket with a stapler. If you want, use a strip of fabric or ribbon to tie a bow around the handle. Line your basket with tissue paper. Fill it with goodies.

ASSEMBLAGE

133

Collect objects with interesting shapes and textures, and assemble them to make a unique sculpture.

What You'll Need: Household objects, shoe box lid, craft glue, poster paint and paintbrush (optional)

Look around your house for a variety of objects such as empty spools, buttons, and paper clips. Try to find items in different sizes, shapes, and textures. You might look for all round items, all long items, or all rough and smooth items. Once you have gathered the objects, assemble them in a design on the inside of a shoe box lid. Try for balance in shapes, textures, or size throughout the arrangement. After your design is in place, glue the objects to the lid. If you want, paint everything in one color before you glue them to the lid to add emphasis to your design.

SCRAPBOOK BINDING

Save memories from a vacation, jot down your thoughts, or sketch drawings in your own special book.

What You'll Need: Two 11×2-inch pieces of cardboard (for the panel), two 11×12-inch pieces of cardboard (for the covers), two 17×20-inch pieces of cloth, ruler, blunt scissors, old paintbrush, craft glue, typing or construction paper, hole punch, yarn

1. Using the illustration as your guide, place 1 cardboard panel piece and 1 cardboard cover piece on 1 piece of cloth. Leave a ¼-inch space between the cardboard pieces. Cut out the corners from the cloth.

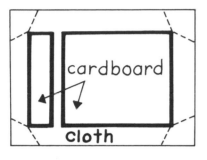

Place cardboard on cloth.

2. Remove the cover board from its position, and apply an even coat of glue on one side of the board. Place it back onto the cloth to glue it in place. Repeat with the panel board. Fold the cloth over the boards and glue in place. Let the glue set.

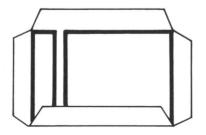

Fold cloth over cardboard.

3. Cut a 7×7-inch square from a piece of paper. Glue the square of paper over the cloth edges on the cover board.

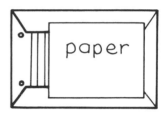

Glue a square of paper over cloth edges.

4. Repeat steps 1 through 3 to make the other cover.

5. Punch 2 holes in the panel of the front and back covers, making sure they line up together. To make the inside pages, punch 2 holes in several sheets of typing or construction paper in the same position as the cover holes. Tie the scrapbook together using yarn.

Tie pieces together.

ANEMOMETER

135 *Measure the wind's strength and make a pretty outdoor decoration, too.*

What You'll Need: Hole punch, 39-ounce-size plastic coffee can lid, blunt scissors, clean plastic egg carton, stapler and staples, yarn, ⅜-inch wood dowel, electrician's tape, clean foam food tray (from fruits and vegetables only)

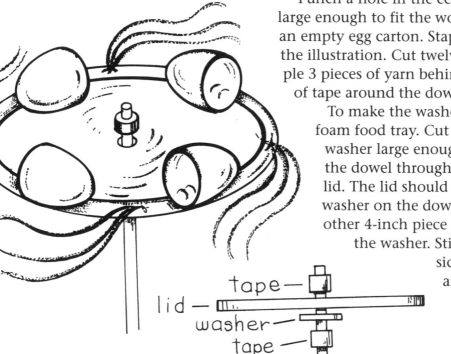

Punch a hole in the center of the plastic coffee can lid large enough to fit the wood dowel. Cut out 4 cups from an empty egg carton. Staple the cups to the lid as shown in the illustration. Cut twelve 6-inch strips of yarn, and staple 3 pieces of yarn behind each cup. Roll a 4-inch piece of tape around the dowel about 2 inches from the end.

To make the washer, cut a 1-inch circle from the foam food tray. Cut a small hole in the center of the washer large enough to fit through the dowel. Place the dowel through the center hole on the plastic lid. The lid should be just below the tape. Place the washer on the dowel under the plastic lid. Wrap another 4-inch piece of tape around the dowel under the washer. Stick the dowel in the ground outside your house in a windy place and watch the anemometer turn.

tape —
lid —
washer —
tape —

PAPER WEAVING

136

Go ahead! Make waves as well as zigzags and curves—all with one fun and colorful paper-weaving technique.

What You'll Need: Assorted colors of construction paper, blunt scissors, ruler, craft glue (optional)

Cut out several 1-inch strips from different-colored sheets of construction paper, lengthwise. Fold another piece of construction paper in half. Starting at the fold, cut straight, zigzag, or curvy lines about 1 inch apart to 1 inch from the edge of the paper. Open the paper, and weave each paper strip over and under each cut. Alternate colors of strips as you weave. Continue weaving until the paper is full. Trim the strips. If you want, glue your paper weaving on a larger piece of paper and hang it on the wall.

DRIED FLOWERS

137

Big bouquets can be used as door decorations or table centerpieces. Tiny bouquets can decorate hats or jewelry.

What You'll Need: Flowers, rubber band, string, hanger, watercolor paints, paintbrush, dish detergent, vase or ribbon

With an adult's permission, gather some flowers from outside. Collect ones that are not quite in full bloom. Gather the stems together and bind them with a rubber band. Thread a piece of string through the rubber band and tie it in a loop. Place the loop over a hanger and hang the bouquet of flowers in the sun upside down. Bring them in at night so dew doesn't collect on them in the morning. Put them back in the sun the next day. They should be dry in about a week. If the sun has bleached out some of the colors, touch the flowers up with watercolor paints. Add a few drops of dish detergent to the paint water to help the paint stick to the flowers. Arrange your bouquet in a vase, or tie a ribbon around it and hang it on the door.

MINIATURE EASEL

138

Display different art projects as often as you like with a craft stick easel.

What You'll Need: Newspaper, acrylic paints, paintbrush, 5 craft sticks or frozen treat sticks, craft glue, cardboard

Cover your work surface with newspaper. Decorate the craft sticks with acrylic paints. Let the paint dry. Glue 3 sticks in the shape of an *A*. Glue a fourth stick sideways to the crosspiece to make the art stand. To make a hinge, have an adult cut a 1-inch square from the cardboard. Fold the square in half. Glue the cardboard to the back of the point of the A-frame. Glue the last stick to the other side of the cardboard. Let the glue set. Stand the easel up, and put your pictures on display.

STRETCH AND WRECK CARS

139

Invent a car with a pool in the back seat, or design a futuristic car. Let your imagination go full speed.

What You'll Need: Old magazines and car advertisements, blunt scissors, drawing or construction paper, craft glue, markers

Cut out cars and other vehicles from magazines and ads. Cut the cars into separate pieces. Then mix and match the pieces to make your own imaginary vehicle. Glue the pieces together on a piece of drawing or construction paper. Add more door parts between the front and back of a car to make a "limo." Glue extra-big tires on a small car. Add a bus front to a luxury car back. Glue the different parts together to create crazy stretch and wreck cars. Draw a scene around your vehicle.

SEASHELL FRAME

140

Collect shells along the shore to decorate a picture frame. Put a photo of you playing at the beach inside the frame.

What You'll Need: Seashells, plain wooden picture frame or wooden box (available at craft stores), craft glue or epoxy

Find a variety of small seashells. Glue them on the picture frame. Start in the corners and make the same arrangement in each one. Then glue small shells between the corner decorations. Let the glue set, then put your picture in the frame. You can also decorate a wooden box with seashells. Just glue the shells on the lid. Give your seashell frame or box as a gift to a friend or family member.

DIORAMA

141

A diorama is a miniature 3-dimensional scene with figures or other objects arranged against a painted background.

What You'll Need: Newspaper, shoe box, poster paints, paintbrush, blunt scissors, construction paper, craft glue

Cover your work surface with newspaper. Make a jungle scene on the inside walls of your shoe box. Paint the ceiling blue and the floor brown. Let the paint dry. Cut out trees with a tab at the bottom from construction paper. Cut a small slit in the center of the tab. Fold each tab piece in the opposite direction, and glue the trees standing in the jungle. Put some trees in the back and some in the front of the box to create depth. Cut out jungle animals such as lions, snakes, and monkeys, and glue them in place.

RECYCLED JEWELS

142

Take apart several pieces of old jewelry, and combine them to re-create your own jewelry for special occasions.

What You'll Need: Old costume jewelry (or buy rhinestones and other faux gems at a craft store), jewelry glue (for plastic and metal), scissors, plastic coffee can lids, metal barrettes or brooch pins

Have an adult help you with this project. Ask your mother and grandmother for some old costume jewelry. With an adult's help, take apart the rhinestones, beads, and pearls. Cut a circle or a unique shape from a plastic coffee can lid. Arrange your "jewels" in a new jewelry design. Glue them to the plastic base, covering the whole piece. Glue a metal barrette or brooch pin to the back of the jewelry base. Let the glue set.

RING TOSS

143

This is a great game to play at birthday parties. And you can tell everyone you made it yourself.

What You'll Need: 2 paper towel tubes, one 12-inch-square piece of foam core or cardboard, masking tape, construction paper, scissors, permanent markers, 3 plastic coffee can lids

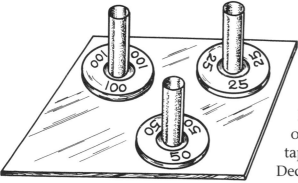

Have an adult help you with this project. To make the ring toss base, cut 2 paper towel tubes in half. Discard 1 half. Tape the remaining 3 tubes to the 12-inch square piece of foam core or cardboard as shown. Cut out 3 circles from a piece of construction paper. Cut a hole out of the center of each circle large enough to fit a towel tube through. Draw the point values on each circle. Place each circle over a tube, covering the masking tape. Cut out the centers of each coffee can lid to make the rings. Decorate each rim with permanent markers. To play, place the ring toss base flat on the floor, and throw the rings over the tubes.

SEED COLLAGE

144

When you recycle seeds from fruits and vegetables, it's as if you're growing a beautiful piece of artwork.

What You'll Need: Dry seeds (from fruits, vegetables, or plants), paper plates, construction paper, craft glue, markers (optional)

Gather seeds from melons, squash, pumpkins, and other fruit. Look for different colors. Wash the seeds. Spread the seeds out on a paper plate and place it in a sunny window. They should be dry in a few days. Once the seeds are dry, use them to create a collage. Apply lines of glue to a piece of construction paper. Sprinkle the seeds over the glue. Let the glue dry. Shake off the excess seeds. Continue gluing and adding seeds to your collage. Try sprinkling white pumpkin seeds with black watermelon seeds to create a contrasting design. You can also use markers to make part of the picture, and then add the seeds to fill it in.

AIRPLANE FLYER

145

Hang your airplane from the ceiling. If you use fishing line, it looks as if the plane is really flying.

What You'll Need: Pencil or black felt-tip pen, clean foam food trays (from fruits or vegetables only), craft knife, permanent markers, craft glue, masking tape

Refer to the illustration and draw the body, wings, and tail pieces of an airplane on a clean foam food tray. With an adult's help, cut out the pieces with a craft knife. Decorate them with permanent markers. Cut 2 slots in the body of the plane for the wings and the tail. Insert the wings and tail, adding a dot of glue to hold them in place. Now you're ready to test-fly your plane. If you need a weight adjustment in the nose or tail, use some masking tape to add the weight.

BIRD FEEDING STATION

146

Turn a plastic bottle into something useful—a place for birds to feast.

What You'll Need: Plastic 2-liter bottle (without a base cap), blunt scissors, nail, 12-inch wood dowel, strong cord, bird seed

Soak the bottle in warm water to remove the label. With an adult's help, use a nail to carefully poke a hole in each side of the plastic bottle near the bottom for the perch. Make sure the holes are large enough to fit the dowel. Cut 2 U-shaped cuts 2 inches above each perch hole. Bend them outward like a little awning. Punch 2 holes just under the top rim of the bottle for the hanger. Thread a piece of strong cord through the holes to hang the feeder. Insert the dowel through the perch holes. Fill the feeder with bird seed, and put the cap back on the bottle. Hang the bird feeder outside, and watch the birds eat.

TISSUE PAPER PASTEUP

147

Don't be too careful when you're tearing tissue paper. Your goal is to make soft, fuzzy shapes that blend.

What You'll Need: Colored tissue paper, drawing paper, pencil, craft glue, old paintbrush, blunt scissors

Tear colored tissue paper into many pieces. Set the torn paper aside. Draw several egg shapes on a piece of drawing paper. Mix equal parts of water and craft glue together. "Paint" the mixture on each shape. Now place torn tissue paper pieces on each shape over the glue. Coat the tissue paper with the diluted glue. Let it dry. The tissue paper creates a bright and fuzzy "paint" for your eggs. Cut the eggs from the paper, and hang them up for Easter decorations.

LEAF PRINTING

148

Gather leaves to print a pattern or design on notecards. It's surprising how pretty your picture will be.

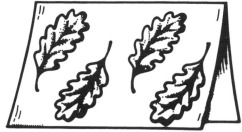

What You'll Need: Newspaper, light-colored construction paper, fresh leaves, acrylic paints, paintbrush, scrap paper

Cover your work surface with newspaper. To make a notecard, fold a piece of construction paper in half. Brush a coat of paint on the back of a leaf. Place the leaf, paint side down, on the front of the notecard. Put a piece of scrap paper over the leaf, and smooth the paper over with your hand. Remove the paper, and carefully peel back the leaf. Let the paint dry. Use more leaves and different colors to create interesting patterns. Continue leaf printing to make more notecards.

HATS: WILD & STYLED

149

Old birthday or holiday wrapping paper makes great dress-up hats for Halloween or just for fun.

What You'll Need: Wrapping paper, blunt scissors, craft glue, old paintbrush, balloon or large ball, trims such as feathers, ribbons, or rhinestones

Make a serious hat for parties, a silly hat just for laughs, or a theme hat for a costume. Cut out 2 big, identical circles of wrapping paper. Mix equal parts of water and glue together. Coat the wrong side of one piece of wrapping paper with glue. Place the other piece, wrong side down, over the glue. Place it on your head and form it into a hat shape while the glue is still wet. Once you've shaped the hat, place it over a blown-up balloon or a ball. Let it set overnight. When it's dry, decorate it with feathers, ribbons, glitter, or rhinestones.

150 ROLLED PAPER BEADS

Rolled paper beads are colorful and shiny—perfect for making tons of beautiful necklaces and bracelets.

What You'll Need: Old magazines, pencil, ruler, blunt scissors, craft glue, yarn or dental floss, newspaper, acrylic spray

1. Cut out 2 or 3 colorful pages from a magazine. Use a ruler to mark an inch along the long edge of a magazine page. Continue making inch marks along the page. Starting at the first 1-inch mark, cut a long triangle from the magazine page. Repeat until you have 20 to 30 triangles.

2. Starting with the wide end of the triangle, roll it around a pencil. Continue rolling until you reach the point of the triangle. Place a dot of glue at the point. Slide the paper bead off the pencil. Repeat until you've made 20 to 30 beads, depending on how long you want your necklace to be.

3. String the beads on yarn or dental floss. Tie the ends together in a double knot. Spread newspaper over your work surface, and place the necklace on the newspaper. With an adult's help, spray acrylic sealer to give your beads a shiny finish.

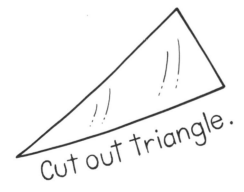

Cut out triangle.

Roll a triangle onto a pencil.

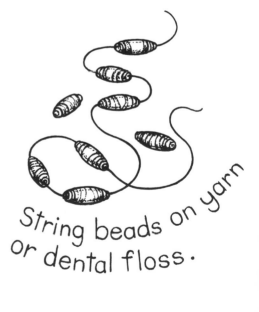

String beads on yarn or dental floss.

151 MILK JUG ANIMALS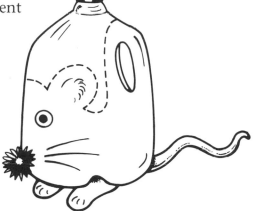

Invent your own animal containers. Create silly features using paper rolls, chenille stems, pom-poms, or yarn.

What You'll Need: Plastic milk jug, pencil, scissors or craft knife, permanent markers, craft glue, black pom-pom, scraps of pink and gray felt, poster board or cardboard

Make a mouse from a clean plastic milk jug. Draw a cut line on the jug as shown. Then with an adult's help, cut out the top part of the jug. Leave the handle on to carry your container. Draw on the mouse's eyes and whiskers. Glue on a black pom-pom for the nose. Cut 2 small semicircles from a scrap of pink felt. Glue 1 on each ear. Cut a long tail from the gray felt, and glue it to the back of the jug at the bottom. Draw paws on a piece of poster board, and have an adult cut them out. Glue the paws to the bottom of the jug.

RECYCLED MAGNETS 152

Redecorate old refrigerator magnets to hold up important school papers, special paintings, or party invitations.

What You'll Need: Markers, poster board or thin cardboard, blunt scissors, flat plastic magnets or magnet strips (available at craft stores), craft glue

Draw musical instruments on a piece of poster board or cardboard. Draw a guitar, a saxophone, or piano keys. Cut out each instrument and color them in wild colors. If you have flat, rectangular plastic magnets, you can make new "covers" for them. Glue the instruments to the top of the flat plastic magnets. If you have a magnetic strip, cut a small piece and glue it to the back of the instrument. Display your new magnets on the refrigerator.

153

SELF-PORTRAITS

If a close friend or grandparent lives far away, make a self-portrait and mail it to them. It's better than a photograph!

What You'll Need: Grocery bags or a roll of brown mailing paper, masking tape, markers, yarn and fabric scraps (optional)

Unroll a long sheet of mailing paper, or cut up 2 or 3 grocery bags and tape them together end to end. Place the sheet down and tape it to hold it in place. Lie down on the paper and have a friend or a family member trace around your body. Now decorate your outline with markers. If you want, glue on yarn for your hair and fabric scraps for your clothes. Make yourself into anything you want. You can be yourself, an astronaut, or a ballerina. Roll up the paper and send it in the Mailing Tube on page 144.

KITCHEN COLLECTION ART

154

It's hard to believe that such a beautiful picture started out as odds and ends headed for the garbage can.

What You'll Need: Plastic cup, markers, collection of throwaway items such as bottle caps, string, or rubber bands, craft glue, construction paper or cardboard

Place a plastic cup in the kitchen to collect all kinds of throwaway items. Label your cup "Kitchen Collection" so that everyone knows to put the items in the cup. Once the cup is full, take a look at what you have collected. Arrange and glue the objects into an interesting collage on a piece of construction paper or cardboard. You'll have so much fun collecting the items that you may want to put a cup in the laundry room and your bedroom for other kinds of objects.

FEATHER PAINTING

Feathers are good for the inside of pillows, to tickle your friend's nose, and to make great paintings!

What You'll Need: Newspaper, 3 feathers (available at craft stores), India ink, poster paints, clean foam food trays (from fruits or vegetables only), drawing paper, scissors or craft knife

Cover your work surface with newspaper. Pour a bit of India ink on a clean foam food tray, and pour some poster paints in another tray. Paint a picture on a piece of drawing paper with one part of each feather: the quill end, the feather tip, and the feather web (edge). Dip the quill end in ink to create sharp lines, dots, and points. Dip the feather tip and the feather web in poster paint to create soft, sweeping lines.

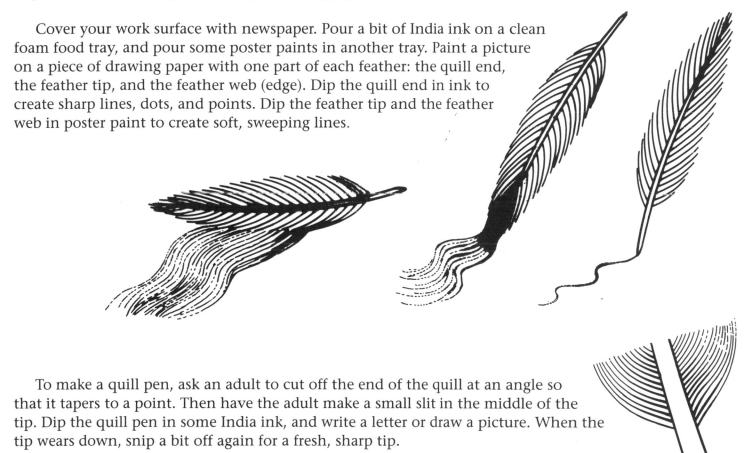

To make a quill pen, ask an adult to cut off the end of the quill at an angle so that it tapers to a point. Then have the adult make a small slit in the middle of the tip. Dip the quill pen in some India ink, and write a letter or draw a picture. When the tip wears down, snip a bit off again for a fresh, sharp tip.

FELT STORYBOARDS

156

Turn a pizza box into a storyboard, and bring the story to life with felt pictures.

What You'll Need: Unused medium-size pizza box, assorted colors of felt, blunt scissors, craft glue, markers, trims (chenille stems, straw, yarn, etc.), resealable plastic bags

To make the storyboard background, cut 2 pieces of dark-colored felt to fit the inside of the top and bottom of the pizza box. Apply a layer of glue to the inside top and bottom of the box. Place both felt background pieces down in the box over the glue. Let the glue dry completely.

Using assorted colors of felt, cut out felt pieces to make a picture. For example, if you were telling the story of *The Three Little Pigs,* you would need 3 pig cutouts, 1 wolf cutout, and 3 house cutouts. Draw features on the pieces with markers. Draw the eyes, noses, and mouths on the pigs. Glue a small piece of curled chenille stem for the tail, and glue on cutout felt overalls. Draw in the eyes, nose, mouth, and teeth on the wolf. Decorate each house with markers, felt, and other trims. Glue or draw straw on one house, some twigs on another house, and red felt bricks on the last house. Place your pieces on the felt background to tell your story. When you're done playing with the storyboard, store each set of pieces in a plastic bag and place the bags in your pizza box.

FAN-TASTIC

157

On the next hot summer day, create your own gentle, cooling breeze with a pretty paper fan.

What You'll Need: Construction paper, blunt scissors, ruler, transparent tape or stapler and staples, pastel chalks or markers

Cut a 6×12-inch piece of construction paper. Draw a picture on the paper using pastel chalks or markers. Draw pretty butterflies, yummy birthday cakes, or stars in a deep blue sky. Now fold the paper back and forth in a fanfold. To start the fanfold, fold one end over about 1 inch. Turn the paper over and fold the end up. Continue folding the paper in accordionlike pleats. Once you've finished folding, staple or tape the folds together at one end to hold it in place. Make bigger fans to decorate your room.

PAPER MAKING

158

Learn the basics of paper making to create pretty, textural paper for art projects or stationery.

What You'll Need: Junk mail or newspaper, dishpans, blender, 8×8-inch piece of small-holed screening, towels, smooth board (to press the paper), cotton cloth

Tear up junk mail envelopes (without the windows), old letters, or newspaper into small pieces. Soak them in a dishpan with warm water overnight. The next day, add more warm water to the paper, and hand-beat the mixture until the pulp is broken apart. Or use a blender to mix it. Place the soaked paper in a blender, and fill it half full with water. With an adult's help, blend it in short bursts to break the pulp up.

Spread some pulp evenly on the screen. The screen should be covered with the paper pulp. Place the screen on a towel. Press a board down hard on the paper to squeeze out any excess water. Remove the board. Place a piece of cotton cloth on a flat surface. Turn the screen over onto the cloth to remove the paper. Let the paper dry.

STAINED GLASS HEART

159

The contrast between a black background and colored tissue paper makes your design pop out.

What You'll Need: Black construction paper, light-colored pencil or chalk, blunt scissors, colored tissue paper, craft glue

Fold a piece of black construction paper in half. Draw half of a heart shape along the fold. Draw shapes inside the heart to cut out. Cut out the heart shape as well as the inside shapes. Glue different colors of tissue paper on the back of the paper, covering the inside cutout shapes. Hang your stained glass paper heart in a window so that the light shines through it. You can also make stained glass paper snowflakes. See the Paper Snowflakes project on page 86 to make the snowflake shapes.

DESK SET

160

With a little imagination, you can recycle ordinary boxes and cans into a matching desk set.

What You'll Need: Empty cereal box, fabric pieces (in colors to match your room), scissors, craft glue, old paintbrush, clean orange juice can, cigar box or small shoe box

To make an "in" box for your desk, have an adult cut an 8½×11-inch piece out of one side of an empty cereal box. Have an adult cut a piece of fabric to fit the outside of the cereal box. Mix equal parts of water and glue. Coat the wrong side of the fabric with the diluted glue, and press it down on the cereal box.

Make the orange juice can into a pencil holder. Have an adult cut a piece of fabric to fit around the can. Coat the fabric with diluted glue, and place it around the can. The cigar box can hold paper clips, rubber bands, and scissors. Cut a piece of fabric to fit the outside of the cigar box. Coat the fabric with glue, and press it down on the box.

FABRIC FRUIT

161

Fabric fruit makes a pretty table decoration, especially when you put it in a handmade bowl.

What You'll Need: Red, yellow, orange, purple, and green felt or cotton cloth, ruler, blunt scissors, fabric glue, yarn, cotton batting, green construction paper, markers

1. To make round fruit, cut an 8×11-inch piece of felt or cotton cloth. Bring the short ends together to make a tube and glue them in place. To make a banana, bring the long ends together to make a tube.

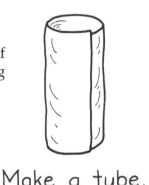

Make a tube.

3. Turn the fabric inside out. Stuff it with cotton batting. Twist the other end and tie it with yarn to close it.

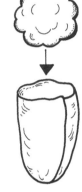

Turn fabric inside out, and stuff with cotton.

2. Twist one end and tie it closed with yarn.

Tie one end with yarn.

4. Cut a leaf shape from a piece of green construction paper. Tuck one end of the leaf into the yarn. If you want, draw decorations on your fruit with markers. Make more round fruit with different colors of fabric, and arrange them in a bowl. (See the Coiled Bowl on page 15.)

Tuck a paper leaf into the yarn.

FAMILY FLAG

162

A family is a team, and every team needs a flag. Make a team flag for your family, and hang it high.

What You'll Need: One 8×12-inch piece of felt, ruler, assorted colors of felt scraps, blunt scissors, craft glue, 18-inch wood dowel with a ¼-inch diameter

Cut out a V-shape at one 8-inch end of the felt. Make a pocket for the dowel at the other short end of the felt. Apply a line of glue along the end of the felt, and fold over 1 inch. Let the glue dry.

To make a coat of arms for your family flag, cut a shield shape from felt. Glue the felt shield to the center of the flag. Cut up other shapes of felt to glue on the shield shape. Think of things your family likes to do. If you like to go camping, cut a tent shape. Glue these other shapes to the shield shape. Let the glue dry, and then insert the dowel in the pocket. If you want, add a tassel to the top of the dowel. See Terrific Tassels on page 210 to make a tassel.

SAND JARS

163

If you think sand belongs at the beach, think again. This project lets you turn ordinary sand into artwork.

What You'll Need: Newspaper, sand, small dishes, powdered poster paints, clean glass jar with lid, acrylic paints, paintbrush

Cover your work surface with newspaper. Mix small amounts of sand with different colors of powdered poster paints in small dishes. Carefully pour one color at a time into a glass jar. Tilt the jar and add about ½ inch of one color of sand. Tilt the glass the other way and add another ½ inch of sand using a different color. Keep tilting the glass and alternating colors until the jar is full. Decorate the lid of the jar with acrylic paints. When the paint is dry, place the lid on the jar. Be careful not to shake your sand picture.

TINY PAPER FLOWERS

164

Make small bouquets with tissue paper and toothpicks. Use these tiny treasures to decorate birthday presents, create floral jewelry, or trim craft projects.

What You'll Need: Blunt scissors, colored tissue paper, toothpicks, craft glue

To make a tiny primrose, cut eight ¼×1½-inch strips of tissue paper. Wrap one end of 4 strips around the toothpick about ¼ inch from the end. Wrap one end of the remaining 4 strips around the toothpick about ½ inch from the end. Fold the "petals" back. To make a tiny daisy, cut several ¾×3-inch strips of tissue paper. Use scissors to round off one end of each strip. Wrap and glue the uncut ends of the strips around a toothpick. To make a lily, cut a half circle from the tissue paper. Wrap the circle around the toothpick like a cone. Glue in place.

RIBBON BASKET

165

Create an all-occasion basket using white ribbons, or select colored ribbons for holiday centerpieces.

What You'll Need: 8½ yards of 1-inch-wide ribbon, cardboard box (from a small bakery cake), aluminum foil, straight pins, craft glue, old paintbrush

1. Cut the ribbon into twelve 18-inch strips. Place 6 strips on your work surface side by side, vertically. Take a separate strip and starting at about 5 inches from one end of the vertical strips, weave it over and under each ribbon horizontally. Repeat with the remaining 5 ribbons. When you are done weaving, the woven part should be centered with the ribbon ends loose.

2. Line a small cardboard box with aluminum foil. Carefully place the ribbon weave in the box. Pin down the bottom to hold it in place. Put the loose ribbon ends up over the sides of the box. Cut three 29-inch pieces of ribbon. Weave one piece over and under to form the first row of the sides. Hold in place with pins. Tuck in any excess ribbon. Weave another piece for the next row. Weave the last piece for the third row. Tuck in the ends and pin in place.

3. Mix equal parts of water and glue. Apply a coat of the diluted glue all over the woven ribbons. Once the glue dries, the ribbon should be stiff. Gently peel it from the foil, and admire your basket.

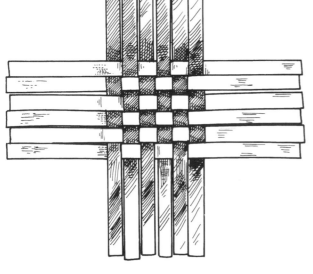

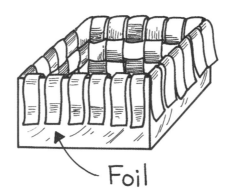

Foil

166 MOSAIC ART

A mosaic is a realistic picture or an abstract design made up of small colored pieces placed side by side.

What You'll Need: Assorted colors of construction paper, blunt scissors, ruler, pencil, drawing paper, craft glue

Make a picture from cut-up pieces of paper. Cut assorted colors of construction paper into ½-inch squares. The easiest way to do this is to gather a stack of same-color papers, measure and mark ½-inch increments on the top sheet, then cut the ½-inch-wide strips. Gather the strips and snip them into squares. Continue with the other colors, keeping the colors separate.

Draw an outline of a simple picture on a piece of drawing paper. Start by covering the outline of your picture with the paper squares. Glue the squares down one by one, leaving a little space between each piece. Then fill in the design and the background, following the shape of your outline.

BEADS & BAUBLES 167

Turn common household items into fashionable jewelry. Just a few items are all you need to make a special necklace for a friend.

What You'll Need: Plastic drinking straws, permanent markers, blunt scissors, ruler, clean foam food tray (from fruits or vegetables only), yarn or embroidery floss

Color several drinking straws with permanent markers. Cut them into ¼-, ½-, and 1-inch lengths. Cut a few circles as well as some other shapes from foam food tray. Decorate them with markers. Punch a hole in the center of each foam bead. String the straws and foam beads on colored yarn or embroidery floss. (If you put a bit of tape around one end of the yarn, it makes it easier to string.) Tie the ends of the yarn or floss together in a bow.

CORNER BOOKMARKS

168

When Mom calls you for dinner and it's time to stop reading, use your own bookmark to hold your place.

What You'll Need: Junk mail envelopes, blunt scissors or pinking shears, markers or colored pencils, scrap of felt, craft glue

Cut the corners from the envelopes of your junk mail. For a straight edge, use scissors to cut the corners. If you want a zigzag edge, use pinking shears. Decorate each corner triangle with markers or colored pencils. Draw on eyes, ears, whiskers, and a nose to make a bookmark mouse. Cut a little tail from a scrap of felt, and glue it to the back of the bookmark. If you cut a wavy edge on the corner triangle, draw a sea scene on the bookmark. Draw waves and a sailboat. Place the triangle bookmark on a page corner to mark your place in your book.

FUNNY ROCK

169

Design a paperweight that will make you rock and roll with laughter every time you look at it.

What You'll Need: Smooth, round rock, blunt scissors, craft glue, newspaper comics, clear nail polish, waxed paper

Find a very round and smooth rock. Cut out your favorite cartoon characters from the newspaper. Apply an even coat of glue to the back of the comic strips. Then place them on the rock. Cover it completely, overlapping the pictures. Once the glue has dried, paint over the whole rock with clear nail polish. The polish creates a clear shellac and seals the pictures. Set the rock on a sheet of waxed paper. Let the polish dry.

FLAPPING BIRD

170

*Time flies when you're making these unique birds.
It's so much fun, why not make a whole flock!*

What You'll Need: Foam core board, pencil, craft knife, markers, ruler, nylon fishing line, blunt scissors, 12-inch dowel, small bead

Draw a bird body and 2 wings on the foam core board. Have an adult help you cut out the pieces with a craft knife. Color the foam pieces with markers to make a dove, flamingo, eagle, or parrot. Poke 2 holes in the side of the bird body. Poke 2 holes at the end of each wing, the same width apart as the 2 holes on the bird body. Poke 2 more holes about ⅓ of the way down each wing.

To connect the wings to the body, thread a piece of fishing line through one end hole of one wing. Continue threading the fishing line through 1 hole on the bird body and on through to an end hole on the other wing. Bring the ends of the fishing line together and tie a knot. Repeat for the other end hole on the wings. Thread a piece of fishing line through each wing hole, and knot the end. Tie the other ends of each fishing line to the dowel. To hang the bird, tie a line from one end of the dowel to the other.

To make the pull string, poke a small hole at the bottom of the bird body. Cut a 10-inch piece of fishing line. Thread it through the bottom hole. Thread a small bead on the end of the line. Tie a knot under the bead to secure it. Pull the line to flap the wings.

STICK WREATH

171

Hang your natural wreath on the front door. It will be a welcome symbol to all who visit your home.

What You'll Need: 10 long, thin branches, large tub or bucket (to soak sticks), silver cord, dried flowers (see Flower Press on page 232)

Find about 10 long, thin branches in your yard. Soak them in warm water overnight. The branches will become soft so that you can bend them. The next day, twist and braid the branches together in a circle. Overlap several branches around the circle of sticks to secure it. Bring the branch ends together, and overlap them. Tie a piece of silver cord around the ends to hold the wreath in place. Tie more silver cord in a few spots around the wreath. Tuck dried flowers into the branches.

TRACING HORSES

172

This project shows all the ways you can "see" a horse—realistic, imaginary, colorful, or fuzzy.

What You'll Need: Book or magazine with horses, tracing paper, pencil, coloring tools such as markers, crayons, colored pencils, or pastel chalks, felt, blunt scissors, craft glue, poster board

Look through a book or a magazine to find a picture of a horse. Using tracing paper and a pencil, trace the horse shape several times. Now use different coloring tools to decorate the horses. Color one in with crayons and use chalk to fill in another one. You can even cut and glue felt to cover one of the horses. Use as many different mediums to color your pictures as you can. Be creative with your colors, too. Your horses can be red and orange, or they can have purple and green stripes. Cut all your new horses out, and glue them into a poster picture on a piece of poster board.

PATTERN PRINTER

173

Turn a potato into a great printing stamp, and turn ordinary paper into decorative gift wrap, book covers, or stationery.

What You'll Need: Newspaper, potato, knife, ballpoint pen, poster paints, clean foam food tray (from fruits or vegetables only), drawing or brown mailing paper

Cover your work surface with newspaper. Clean a potato, and have an adult help you cut it in half. Draw a shape on the cut surface with a pen. Have an adult cut away the edges so that the shape stands out. Place some poster paint on a clean foam food tray. Dip the potato shape in the paint, and then press it on a piece of paper. Continue stamping the paper until you've created a pattern you like. Let the paint dry.

DOLL BED

174

Make a doll's bed fit for a queen from only a shoe box and some paint.

What You'll Need: Shoe box with lid, scissors or craft knife, ruler, newspaper, poster paints, paintbrush, craft glue

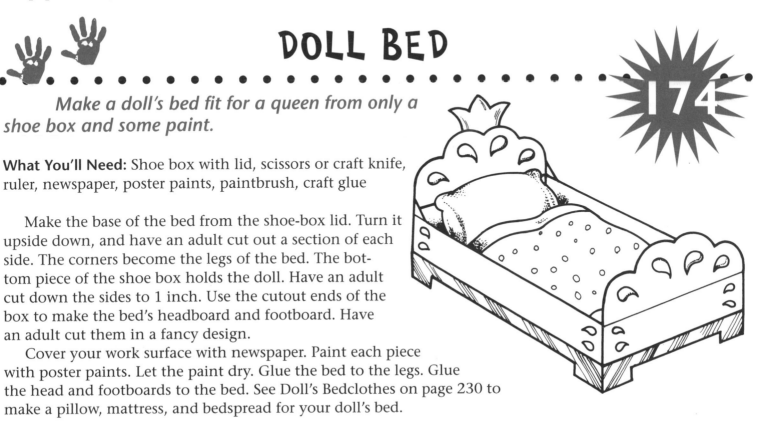

Make the base of the bed from the shoe-box lid. Turn it upside down, and have an adult cut out a section of each side. The corners become the legs of the bed. The bottom piece of the shoe box holds the doll. Have an adult cut down the sides to 1 inch. Use the cutout ends of the box to make the bed's headboard and footboard. Have an adult cut them in a fancy design.

Cover your work surface with newspaper. Paint each piece with poster paints. Let the paint dry. Glue the bed to the legs. Glue the head and footboards to the bed. See Doll's Bedclothes on page 230 to make a pillow, mattress, and bedspread for your doll's bed.

MILK JUG CATCH

175

This is a great game to play indoors or outdoors, and it's especially fun since you made it yourself.

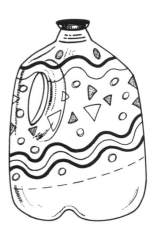

What You'll Need: 2 clean plastic milk jugs, scissors or craft knife, permanent markers, soft foam ball or plastic ball

With an adult's help, cut the bottom off of 2 clean plastic milk jugs as shown. (For an easy game, use gallon jugs. To make the game more challenging, use quart jugs.) Keep the caps on the jugs. Decorate the plastic jugs with permanent markers. To play the game, toss a ball to your partner. He or she catches it in the jug. Then your partner throws it to you. To make the game harder, throw the ball when it is still in the jug. Use a soft foam ball to play the game inside, and use a plastic ball to play outside.

PAPER DOLL CHAIN

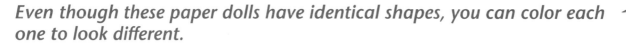

176

Even though these paper dolls have identical shapes, you can color each one to look different.

What You'll Need: Drawing paper, blunt scissors, pencil, markers, trims such as ribbon, yarn, or fabric scraps, craft glue

Fanfold a piece of drawing paper evenly (see Fan-Tastic on page 103 for the folding technique). Draw your design for the paper dolls. Make sure the design touches both sides of the paper so the dolls "hold hands." Draw only one half of the doll since the other half will be across the top fold. Cut out the doll pattern. Then decorate each doll with markers, or glue on trims such as ribbon, yarn, or fabric scraps. You can also make holiday decorations with paper chains of hearts, shamrocks, bunnies, or stars—just remember to leave a part touching each edge.

WIND CHIMES

177

Hang your wind chime outside and listen to its sounds. It's as if the soft breezes are singing to you.

What You'll Need: Plastic coffee can lid, scissors, ruler, string, plastic egg carton, large jingle bells

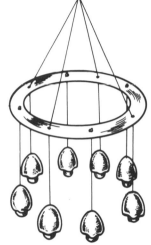

Have an adult help you with the cutting in this project. To make the wind chime ring, cut the center from a plastic coffee can lid. Make sure the ring is at least ½ inch wide. To make the wind chime hanger, punch 4 holes evenly spaced around the ring. Thread a piece of string through each hole. Bring the ends of each string together at the top, and tie them in a knot. Punch 4 more holes between the others. Hang string down from each hole on the ring.

Make egg carton bells for each string. Cut out a cup, and poke a hole in the center. Thread the cup through the hanging string, and tie a jingle bell into each cup.

SPONGE SCULPTURE

178

Build fun soft sculptures that you can even use in the tub! Watch them grow as they absorb water.

What You'll Need: Assorted colors of sponge, fabric glue, blunt scissors

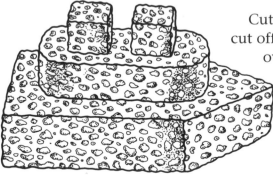

Cut up sponges to make a sponge boat. To make the base of the boat, cut off the corners of one end of a sponge so it comes to a point. Cut an oval shape from another sponge in a different color. Use a third color to cut 2 small squares for the top of the boat. Glue the oval shape on top of the boat base. Glue the 2 small squares on top of the oval shape. The fabric glue allows you to use the sponges in the top without falling apart. Make more sponge sculptures for the tub. Cut out fish shapes—even little hamburgers and hot dogs!

179 FLOWER MAKING FUN

This is a great winter's day project—just as you begin to really miss all the wonderful summer flowers.

What You'll Need: Blunt scissors, construction paper, pipe cleaners, transparent tape, colored tissue paper, plastic egg carton, vase, potpourri (optional)

To make a lily, cut an ice cream cone shape from a piece of construction paper. Overlap the sides of paper together around a pipe cleaner stem. Tape the sides to hold it in place. Bend the top end of the pipe cleaner in a small loop to form the stamen.

To make a rose, cut 3 different-size circles from tissue paper. Place the circles on top of each other and poke a hole in the center. Insert the pipe cleaner through the center, and twist the bottom of the circles. Secure it with a piece of tape.

To make a tulip, cut 1 cup from an empty egg carton. Trim the edges in the shape of a tulip. Poke a small hole in the center of the cup, and insert a pipe cleaner stem. For the daffodil, make a tulip and add a circle of tissue paper around the bottom of the cup.

Once you have made your flowers, arrange them in a vase, and place the vase in your bedroom or on the kitchen table. Ask an adult for some potpourri, and put it inside the vase to add fragrance to your bouquet.

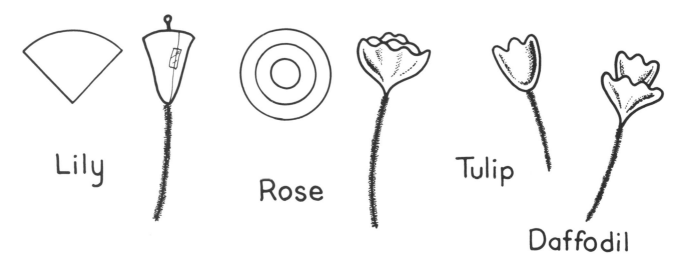

Lily   Rose   Tulip   Daffodil

DRIED APPLE CREATURES

180

Dried apple people make great puppet heads and fun sculptures. At Halloween, hang them from the ceiling as shrunken heads.

What You'll Need: Apples, knife, cloves, lemon juice, salt, yarn, cardboard, trims such as pipe cleaners or fabric scraps (optional)

Ask an adult to help you peel and core an apple. Cut a face in the apple. Set in 2 cloves for the eyes. Mix together 1 part lemon juice, 1 part warm water, and 1 to 2 teaspoons of salt. Dip the whole apple in the mixture to help preserve it. Let it dry in a warm, dry place for a few days. Notice that once it is dry, the apple shrinks and wrinkles, making your face look different from the one you originally cut. Glue on yarn hair and a cardboard hat to decorate your apple creature. If you want, add pipe cleaners to make glasses or antennas, or use fabric scraps for clothes.

PAPER CUTOUTS #2

181

Hang these designs on a Christmas tree, in a window, or from a mobile. You can even paste them on a handmade card.

What You'll Need: Drawing paper, blunt scissors, ruler

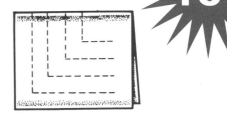

Fold a piece of paper in half. Starting at the fold, cut repeated lines, arches, or L-shapes in the paper as shown. Unfold the paper and bend every other strip outward. Cut an 8-inch circle from a piece of paper. Fold it in half, and then fold it in half again. Starting at the double-fold, cut curved lines along the curve to ½ inch from the single fold. Open it up and bend every other strip—one toward you and one away from you on each side. Experiment with other shapes, and use your paper cutouts for ornaments or mobile decorations.

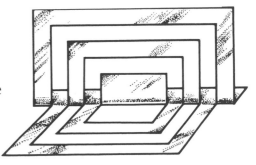

GARDEN MARKERS

182

Now you'll never forget where you planted the carrots! You can even make notes about watering needs and harvest time.

What You'll Need: Permanent markers, plastic milk jugs, scissors or craft knife, garden seeds

Refer to the illustration and draw the cut lines of a square with a spike on a plastic milk jug. With an adult's help, cut out the garden marker shape. Draw the plant's picture shown on your package of garden seeds. Write the name of the plant as well. Add the plastic markers to your garden. You can also make a set of garden markers for your houseplants. Learn all the names and how to care for them, and write the instructions on the plastic markers.

EXPLODING GLIDER

183

Here's a project you can throw together quickly. Just be careful to toss your glider away from other people.

What You'll Need: 6 craft sticks or frozen treat sticks, markers, cardboard (optional)

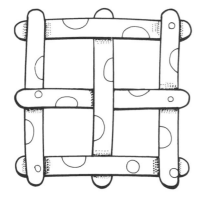

Decorate the sticks with markers. Arrange the sticks in the window pane pattern shown in the illustration. The cross pieces go over and under the outer pieces to provide the tension that holds the sticks together. Now go outside and throw your glider. When you throw it, it explodes! You can make glider games. Draw a big bull's-eye pattern on a piece of cardboard. Place it on the floor. When you throw the glider, add up the points you score as it lands on different sections.

184 CEREAL BOX BOOKBINDING

Create your own journal, scrapbook, or sketchbook. Now you have some place to put precious memories.

What You'll Need: Typing paper, needle and thread, empty cereal box, blunt scissors, ruler, two 9×11-inch pieces of wrapping paper, craft glue, white construction paper

1. Fold 40 sheets of typing paper in half. Separate 8 sheets from the 40, and sew the pages together along the fold using a needle and thread. Repeat with 4 more 8-page sections. Cut the front and back covers from a cereal box. Follow the cut lines shown in the illustration to cut two 6×9-inch pieces with a ½-inch spine.

2. Place a 9×11-inch piece of wrapping paper on your work surface, and cut off the corners as shown. Coat the front cover piece with glue, and place it down on the wrapping paper. Glue the flaps over. Repeat for the back cover.

3. Cut two 5×7-inch pieces of white construction paper. Glue 1 to the inside of each cover piece. Glue the spines of the front and back covers together. Then put glue on the inside spine, and insert the five 8-page sections. Let it set overnight.

Wrapping paper

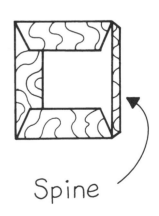

Spine

PAPER LANTERNS

185

String a series of pretty paper lanterns along an outside porch or window. Watch them sway gently in the wind.

What You'll Need: Wrapping paper or construction paper, ruler, blunt scissors, transparent tape

1. Cut a 4×6-inch piece of paper. Fold the rectangle in half lengthwise. Cut slits along the fold about ½ inch apart.

2. Open the paper and tape the short edges together with the fold pointing outward.

3. Cut a strip of paper to make a handle. Tape it across the top of the lantern. Now you can hang your lantern. Make more lanterns so you can hang a series of them outside or in your room.

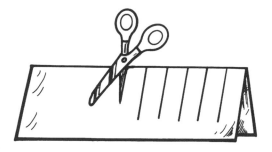

Make cuts in the fold.

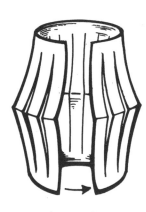

Tape short edges together.

Tape handle across the top of the lantern.

NO-DRAWING DESIGN

186

How can you make a design without drawing? It's easy—just use the sun to "draw" a picture.

What You'll Need: Dark-colored construction paper, household objects

Gather several household objects such as a wrench, a key, or a small bowl. Place a piece of dark-colored construction paper in a sunny spot outside or near a window. Arrange your objects on the paper. Leave the paper in the sunny spot for a week. After a week, remove the objects and you'll notice that the areas where the objects were are darker than the other areas. Now you have a no-drawing design. If you want, add some drawing to your picture to make the objects into something specific such as a person from the wrench or an alligator from the key.

BOX CARS

187

With a few materials and a little imagination, you can make a race car, a sports car, or even a minivan.

What You'll Need: Old boxes, blunt scissors, construction paper, craft glue, markers, plastic milk jug lids or cardboard, clear plastic cup, aluminum foil

Save some small boxes from the kitchen or from gifts about the size of a butter box, a cocoa mix box, or a necklace box. Cover the boxes with different colors of construction paper. Decorate paper-covered boxes with markers. For the wheels, glue on plastic milk jug lids or cut circles from cardboard. Make a windshield from a clear plastic cup cut in half. Glue it to the box. Use aluminum foil to make headlights and bumpers. If you want, cut holes in the top of the boxes for the Clothespin People on page 148. Use them to drive your cars around town.

NATURE BOOKMARK

188

Make a bookmark to remember last summer's garden. Don't forget to include leaves from your vegetable garden as well.

What You'll Need: 2×6-inch piece of fabric, pressed flowers (see Flower Press on page 232), craft glue, fabric markers, 2×12-inch piece of iron-on flexible vinyl, iron and ironing board, blunt scissors

Place fabric flat on your work surface with the right side up. Arrange some pressed flowers on the fabric and glue in place. Add more decoration to your design with fabric markers. Let the glue dry. Place the flexible vinyl on the fabric, and slowly peel the paper backing about 2 to 3 inches down from the vinyl. Place the sticky side of the vinyl down at one end of the bookmark. Peel the paper backing from the vinyl as you press the vinyl in place on the bookmark. Be sure to keep the edges even. Turn the fabric over to continue pressing the vinyl in place on the back of the bookmark. Once the vinyl is in place, put the paper backing, shiny side down, over the vinyl. With an adult's help, press with an iron for 3 to 4 seconds. Remove the paper and allow to cool. Trim the edges with scissors.

ARTS & CRAFTS TO SHARE

Games, gifts, and projects for pretend play make up this chapter. You can work on them with a friend or an adult, or you can work by yourself and share the results! Many of the projects make great family activities—while you're working on one project, your brother or sister can work on another one. Remember, working together can be fun, and doesn't have to be a competition. Work at your own pace and ability level. Help each other choose colors and think of new ideas. Most importantly, use this time to explore yourself, and the experience will be a genuine sharing one between you and your family.

BAG-IT WRAPPINGS

189

If you have an odd-shaped gift that makes traditional wrapping difficult—just bag it!

What You'll Need: Sponges, blunt scissors, newspaper, poster paints, paper plates, plain paper bags, construction paper, stapler and staples

Sponge-print a design on paper bags for gifts. Cut sponges into shapes such as a star, a birthday candle, or geometric figures. Cover your work surface with newspaper. Place some poster paints on paper plates. Dampen one sponge slightly and dip it in the paint. Press the sponge on the paper bag to print your design. Let the paint dry.

To make a handle, fold a piece of construction paper in thirds lengthwise. Staple it to the bag. Now make a matching notecard. Fold a piece of construction paper in half, and sponge on the same design. Cut a slit in the fold of the notecard, and slip it over the handle to close the bag.

AUTO BINGO

190

The next time you take a long car trip, play Auto Bingo. It makes the time fly by.

What You'll Need: Three 10×10-inch pieces of felt, marker, ruler, a large, clean pizza box, craft glue, old magazines, blunt scissors

Use a marker to draw a checkerboard on 2 pieces of felt. Divide these pieces into twenty-five 2-inch squares, drawing lines 2 inches apart down and across. There should be 5 squares down each side. On 1 checkerboard, write "free" in the middle space. Glue this felt piece inside the pizza box on one side and the unmarked third felt piece on the other side.

Look through old magazines for pictures of objects you see when you travel—a mail box, speed limit sign, police car, stoplight, gas station, cow, and so on. You will need 24 pictures. Cut the objects out, making sure they are small enough to fit in a 2-inch checkerboard square. Using the other felt piece with a checkerboard, glue each picture onto a 2-inch square. (If you can't find the pictures you need, just draw the objects on the squares.) Cut out the picture squares and arrange them on the checkerboard felt piece pasted in the box. Fill in all the squares except for the "free" space.

To play bingo, look for the objects on your bingo card when you are taking a car trip. When you see one, remove the picture square from your bingo card. When you have an empty row across, down, or diagonally, you win! To play again, rearrange the picture squares on the felt checkerboard. This way, you create a different game every time you play.

191

GAS PUMP

Add a gas station to your town on the Motor Mat project on page 218 with your own gas pump.

What You'll Need: Markers, paper towel tube, scissors, shoestring

Decorate a paper towel tube with markers. Draw windows for the price and gallons. Add the name of your gas station. Ask an adult to poke 2 holes in the tube: one near the top and one near the bottom. To make the gas hose, thread a shoestring in the bottom hole. Knot the end of the string on the inside. Pull the shoestring up to the top hole for hanging up the "nozzle" (the plastic tip of the shoestring). Now you're ready to fill 'er up!

BEANBAG GAMES

192

You can play lots of different games with beanbags. So get ready, aim, and toss!

What You'll Need: Cardboard box, markers, scissors, poster board, empty coffee can, construction paper, transparent tape, 6 paper towel tubes, beanbags (see Beanbags on page 229)

Make one or all of the following games. Game 1: Draw a face on the bottom of a cardboard box with 2 big eyes and a big mouth. Have an adult cut out the mouth and eyes. To play, throw the beanbags through the holes. Game 2: Draw a tic-tac-toe board on poster board. Toss the beanbags on the board to get three in a row. Game 3: Draw a design on a sheet of construction paper. Tape the paper around a large coffee can. Standing at all different distances from the can, try to toss your beanbags in it. Game 4: Decorate 6 paper towel tubes. Stand them up and try to knock each one down with a toss of a beanbag.

GIANT DICE

193

No more lost dice. These oversized cubes are fun to use and hard to lose!

What You'll Need: Pencil, poster board (at least 8½×6½ inches), blunt scissors, ruler, markers, craft glue

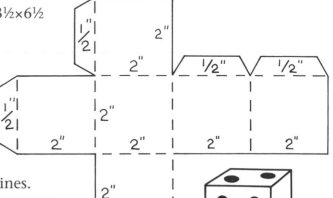

Draw the pattern shown on the poster board. (Make a bigger pattern for larger dice or a gift box.) Be sure to follow the dimensions exactly. Each square is 2 inches on each side; the tabs are ½ inch wide. Cut along the solid lines and score on the dotted lines. Scoring makes it easier to fold the poster board. To score, use a ruler to guide the point of your scissors as you "draw a line" along the dotted lines.

Decorate the 6 squares. Make dots as on regular dice, or draw numbers, letters, or shapes. Make the cutout into a box by folding along the scored lines. Place glue on the tabs and tuck them inside the box to hold it together.

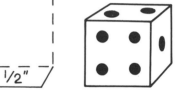

STICK PUPPETS

194

Turn your life story into a play. Make puppets using your baby photos as well as recent photos.

What You'll Need: Photographs of yourself, blunt scissors, craft sticks, craft glue, cardboard box, poster paints, paintbrush, fabric (to cover the box opening)

Find some pictures of yourself from when you were a baby to the present. Ask permission to cut out "yourselves" and glue a craft stick to the back of each photo. Make a box stage to act out your play. Cut out the bottom of the box. Decorate it with paint to make it look like a room in your house. Then tell your own story with your stick puppets. Add a curtain to your stage. Glue a piece of fabric across the top front edge of the box. Pull it back over the top to raise the curtain.

195 A GRANDPARENT'S STORY

When you combine your drawing with a grandparent's story, you create a generational piece of artwork.

What You'll Need: 3×5-inch index cards, construction paper, craft glue, markers or colored pencils, hole punch, yarn, blunt scissors

Make a book about your grandparents. Think of a question and write it on an index card. Try to come up with 8 to 10 questions. You can ask questions such as "What was your favorite toy?" or "Where did you live when you were ten?" Have them write the answer on the card. If your grandparents live far away, mail the cards back and forth. Once you have all the cards, glue each one to the bottom half of a sheet of construction paper. Draw a picture above the card to illustrate your grandparent's answer. Decorate a separate sheet of construction paper for the front cover. To bind your book, set all the pages together and punch 4 holes along the left edge. Cut a piece of yarn, thread it through the holes, and tie it in a bow.

What was your favorite toy?

A train

MAGIC WAND

196

With a wave of the magic wand you can become a magician or even a fairy godmother.

What You'll Need: 2 yards of ribbon, blunt scissors, ruler, craft glue, 24-inch wood dowel with ½-inch diameter, sequins or small jingle bells (optional), cardboard, ballpoint pen or black felt-tip pen, aluminum foil, old paintbrush

Cut a 24-inch piece of ribbon. Glue one end of the ribbon to one end of the wood dowel. Wrap it around the dowel. Once you reach the bottom, trim off the excess ribbon and glue the end in place. To make the wand streamers, cut a few strips of ribbon with varying lengths. Glue one end of each strip to the top end of the dowel. If you want, add some sequins or small jingle bells to each streamer end.

Cut a small strip of cardboard about 1 inch long. Wrap and glue the strip of cardboard around the dowel ½ inch from the top end, covering the ends of the ribbons. Have an adult cut 2 small slits in the cardboard across from each other. Draw and cut out a moon, star, or other magical symbols from the aluminum foil. To stiffen the foil, coat one side with glue and let it dry. Insert the foil shape in the slits. Add a dab of glue to hold it in place.

CHINESE GIFT CARTONS

197

You'll have as much fun making this birthday gift box as you do selecting and giving the present.

What You'll Need: Plain Chinese food cartons, black felt-tip pen, scissors, construction paper or colored tissue paper, craft glue, strip of fabric or ribbon (optional)

If the carton has a handle, carefully pull it off of the carton. Set it aside. Draw a birthday or holiday symbol on each side of the carton. For a birthday present, you might draw a birthday cake or for Christmas, an ornament shape. With an adult's help, carefully cut out the shape. Paste a piece of construction paper or colored tissue paper behind the cutout window. Carefully place the handle back on the carton. If your carton does not have a handle, staple the fabric strip or ribbon to the carton to make a handle.

MOOD MUSIC ART

198

Let the music guide your pencil as you create artwork that matches the mood of the music.

What You'll Need: Radio, drawing paper, coloring tools such as markers, pastel chalks, and colored pencils

Listen to a song on the radio. As you listen to it, draw the way it makes you feel. Use several coloring tools such as markers, pastel chalks, and colored pencils to experiment with colors. Think about the colors you would use with fast, slow, or marching music. After you finish that picture, change the station on the radio to find another song with a different tempo. Draw another picture. Keep experimenting with various types of music. Compare the pictures you made for the different kinds of music such as jazz, country, classical, and rock 'n' roll.

PIPE CLEANER EARS

199

These ears are great for Halloween costumes, birthday parties, or any old day you feel like being silly.

What You'll Need: 6 or 7 pipe cleaners, scissors, construction paper, markers, craft glue, yarn (optional)

Make a hat form with pipe cleaners. To start, twist the ends of 2 or 3 pipe cleaners together in a band. Make sure it fits around your head. Have an adult trim off any excess. Take 4 pipe cleaners and attach them to the band. Twist them together at the top to make a "hat."

Cut 2 rabbit ears in a fold-over pattern from a piece of construction paper. Color them with markers. Fold them over the top pipe cleaners and glue the sides together. To create more pretend "hats," make other animal ears or antennas that stick up or hang from the band, or tie yarn to the pipe cleaners to make a wig.

CRAFT FOAM STAMPERS

200

These stamps are ideal for making holiday greeting cards or invitations to your birthday party.

What You'll Need: Craft foam (available at craft stores), blunt scissors, fabric glue, blocks of wood, poster paints or stamp pads

Cut out shapes from craft foam. Glue each shape on a block of wood. You can make 1 large stamp to decorate the front of a birthday card or small stamps to create repeating shapes on wrapping paper or gift bags. Combine 2 or 3 small shapes on a single block of wood to make interesting repeating patterns. Try hearts, circles, squares, or stars. You can also make letter or word stamps. Cut out letters or words that you want to print, and glue them to a block in a mirror image. Use poster paints or stamp pads to ink your stampers. Wash your stamps after each use.

BALLOON BADMINTON

201

Mom always said not to play ball in the house—until she learned this fun indoor game.

What You'll Need: 2 craft sticks, 2 plastic coffee can lids, craft glue, markers, balloons, newspaper, blunt scissors, string or yarn, 2 chairs

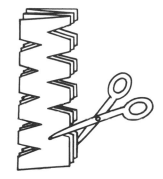

Glue a craft stick to each plastic coffee can lid to make the badminton rackets. Use markers to decorate your rackets with opposing pictures. You might draw a sun on one and a moon on another, or an elephant and a mouse, or a red and green light.

To make the net, fanfold a sheet of newspaper. Cut out V-sections as shown. Open the paper and thread some string through the top row of the cutouts. Tie the net to 2 chairs. Blow up a balloon, and play a slow-motion, fun game of badminton inside the house. If you want, decorate the balloon to match your rackets (this is most easily done before the balloon is filled with air). You might draw a star, a peanut, or a yellow light.

CUT A CASTLE

202

You'll be the ruler of the land in your very own castle.
Make the Clothespin People on page 148 into your royal subjects.

What You'll Need: White cake box, blunt scissors, 4 paper towel tubes, white paper, transparent tape, markers or poster paints and paintbrush, construction paper scraps, craft glue, toothpick

Cut a drawbridge in the side of the clean cake box. Cut out a square from the top of the box. The hole is the opening for the courtyard, and the rim is the base for the battlement. Make 4 towers from the paper towel tubes. Wrap white paper around the tubes, and secure it with tape. Make a cone for the roof of 1 tower. Tape it to the top of a tube. Tape a tower to each corner of the box.

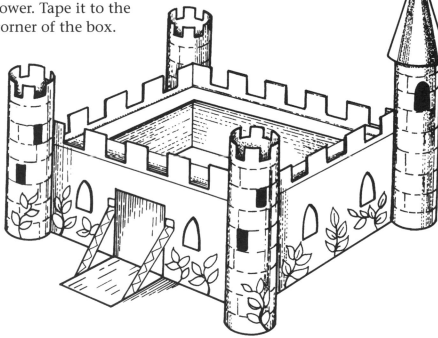

To make the wall around the battlement, cut 4 strips of white paper into a comb shape. Make them long enough for each side of the box. Tape them around the castle's top edge. Use markers or paint to decorate the castle with windows, vines, and bricks. To make a flag for the castle tower, cut a scrap piece of construction paper in a triangle. Glue it to a toothpick. Insert the toothpick in the top of the cone on the tower, and glue it in place.

FANCY FABRIC FRAME

203

Photos help us preserve precious moments. What better way to display them than in their own customized frame?

What You'll Need: Wooden picture frame, paper towels and glass cleaner, printed fabric, craft glue

With an adult's help, carefully remove the glass and backing from the wooden picture frame. Wipe off any dust or smudges from the glass using a paper towel and glass cleaner. Cut strips of printed fabric. Apply glue to the frame, and wrap the strips of fabric around it. Cover the whole frame with fabric strips, smoothing them in place as you wrap it. Trim off any excess fabric, then glue the ends to the back. Let the glue set. Put the frame back together to display your favorite photo.

NO-BORED GAMES

204

Who said studying can't be fun? This dinosaur board game is not only fun—it may even help improve your grades!

What You'll Need: Poster board, scissors, markers, index cards, 6 craft sticks, small plastic cup

On the poster board, draw a snakelike road. Divide it into squares. Color each area with one of 6 colors. Draw dinosaurs, volcanoes, swamps, and tar pits alongside the road. Write "Jump ahead 1" or "Go back 1" on some squares. Draw question marks on 5 squares. On each index card, write a question about dinosaurs. If you land on a question mark, you must answer a question about dinosaurs to move. Make pick sticks to move. Color the bottom 1 inch of each craft stick with one of your 6 colors. Put the sticks, color side down, in the small plastic cup. Draw 1 pick stick to see what color you move to. Customize your game using the Game Pieces on page 149 or the Giant Dice on page 126.

CRAFT STICK PUZZLES

205

Since these puzzle pieces have the same shape, your only clues are designs and colors.

What You'll Need: 12 to 16 craft sticks, transparent tape, markers

Place the craft sticks side by side. You may want to put a piece of tape on one side of the sticks to keep them together while you draw. Draw a picture on the sticks and color it in. To make a two-in-one puzzle, draw another picture on the other side. Remove the tape and turn the sticks over. Add tape to the other side again to hold the sticks in place. Draw the second picture. Now remove the tape and mix up the sticks. Then put your picture back together.

PRETEND STORE

206

Invite your friends over and have each of you design your own store. Together you can make a mini-mall.

What You'll Need: Ruler, scissors, assorted colors of construction paper, clean foam food trays (from fruits or vegetables only), markers, shoe box with lid, craft glue

Have an adult help you with the cutting. Make several different types of stores for your mini-mall. All you need is some play money and a cash register to get started. To make play money, cut several 2½×6-inch pieces from green construction paper. Decorate them to make your own dollar bills. Add the amounts—$1, $5, $10, and even $100. Cut several circles from foam food trays to make the coins. Decorate them with markers.

Make a cash register from a shoe box. Cut the lid in half. Use one half as the cash drawer. Place the lid half back on the box, and turn the box upside down. Pull out one half of the lid and place your play money inside. To make the cash register buttons, cut small circles from different colors of construction paper. Write numbers and words such as "Total" and "Void" on the buttons. Glue them to the box.

Now you're ready to play store. For a grocery store, gather food cartons and boxes. Collect junk mail for a post office. Use stuffed animals for a pet store. Gather old shopping bags for your purchases. Draw your store's sign on a piece of construction paper.

PICTURE PUNS

207

Draw pictures that stand for a word. Have your friends and family guess the words!

What You'll Need: 8 to 11 sheets of drawing paper, markers, stapler

Draw 2 pictures that stand for a word on a sheet of drawing paper. You might choose the word *snowman* and draw snowflakes and a man or *starfish* and draw a star and a fish. Write the word on the back of the paper. Make 8 to 10 picture puns. Make a book out of your drawings. Decorate a sheet of drawing paper for the cover. Set all the pages together and staple the top of the pages to bind your book. Show your book to family members and see if they can guess your words.

Try other picture puns with homonyms. These are words that sound alike but have different spellings and meanings. Some examples are aunt and ant; rein, reign, and rain; and cache and cash. Draw as many as you can and add them to your book.

NO ORDINARY VASE

Display real flowers or pretend flowers that you made with Flower Making Fun on page 116 in this unique vase.

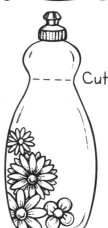

What You'll Need: Plastic dish detergent bottle, blunt scissors, old garden catalogs or floral print wrapping paper, newspaper, craft glue, measuring spoon, old paintbrush, water-based polyurethane, marbles

Clean out the dish detergent bottle thoroughly. Have an adult cut off the top of the bottle. Cut out lots of flower pictures from garden catalogs or from wrapping paper. Cover your work surface with newspaper. Dilute the glue with 2 teaspoons of water. Using a paintbrush, apply the glue to the back of the pictures. Cover the plastic bottle with the pictures. Clean the paintbrush thoroughly. Let the glue dry. To seal the pictures, coat the vase with water-based polyurethane. Arrange real, silk, or pretend flowers in the vase. Experiment with different combinations and color schemes. Put marbles in the bottom of the vase to anchor the stems.

LETTER WRITING KIT

Combined with the Stationery Set on page 55, this kit makes the perfect gift for a friend who has moved away.

What You'll Need: Envelopes, blunt scissors, construction paper, ruled writing paper, craft glue, markers, shoe box, cardboard-covered address book (available at stationery stores), ballpoint pen, ribbon

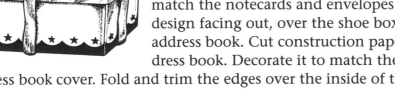

To make notecards and matching envelopes, see the Stationery Set on page 55. Cut a sheet of construction paper to fit the shoe box. Decorate it to match the notecards and envelopes. Glue the construction paper, with the design facing out, over the shoe box. Make a front and back cover for the address book. Cut construction paper slightly larger than the cover of the address book. Decorate it to match the stationery design. Glue the paper over the address book cover. Fold and trim the edges over the inside of the book. Place all the items and a pen in the box. Wrap ribbon around the box and tie in a bow.

CANDLE DISH

210

Create a project that really shines. Brighten up a room or highlight a table with candle dishes.

What You'll Need: Glass bowl or tumbler, permanent markers, round or star-shaped candle (available at craft stores), food coloring (optional)

Decorate the outside of the glass bowl or tumbler—all the way around—with permanent markers. Be sure to let it dry for a few minutes between applications of different colors. Draw stars, snowflakes, or bursts of fireworks. Fill the bowl or tumbler half full with water and float a small candle. If you want, add a drop or two of food coloring to the water. Ask an adult to light the candle. The light will shine through your design.

PUPPET THEATER

211

With this portable puppet stage you can take your show on the road.

What You'll Need: 44×44-inch piece of fabric, needle and thread, measuring tape, two 1×2-inch boards 4 feet long, 8 feet of cord, fabric paints

Fold the fabric in half. Have an adult help you sew the first pocket seam 2 inches below the fold. Then measure 20 inches from the first seam and stitch across the fabric. To make the pocket seam, sew another stitch 2 inches from the previous one. Measure 2½ inches from the top pocket seam, and cut a 25×15-inch hole for the puppets. Decorate the fabric with fabric paint. Let the paint dry. Insert the 1×2-inch boards in each of the 2 pocket seams. Tie the cord from one end of the top bar to the other. Hang the theater in a doorway, or prop the top bar between 2 chairs.

SUSAN'S THEATRE

FIND THE PRESENTS

212

In this game of strategy, race your opponent to locate the hidden presents.

What You'll Need: Drawing paper, ruler, markers, blunt scissors, construction paper

To make the game board, draw an 8×8-inch square on a piece of drawing paper. Divide the square into 64 squares, 1 inch each, by drawing lines 1 inch apart down and across. There should be 8 squares down each side. Label the rows across A through H and label the columns down 1 through 8 as shown. Have an adult take your original to a copy center and make 4 copies—you'll need 4 copies to play 1 game. (Save your original game board to make more copies later.)

On a piece of construction paper, draw 10 presents. Make four 1×2-inch presents, and six 1×1-inch presents. Decorate your presents and cut them out. Each player gets 2 large presents, 3 small ones, and 2 game boards.

To play the game, arrange your presents on 1 game board. Then take turns guessing the location of your opponent's presents by calling out the name of the square. For example, you might ask if the present is in E-3. If the answer is no, mark the E-3 spot on your blank game board with an X; if the answer is yes, mark it with a star. Then your friend takes a turn. The first person to find all the presents wins.

213 CLOTHESPIN MAGNETS

Design your own clothespin magnet to display your art projects or good grades.

What You'll Need: Thin cardboard or poster board; markers; blunt scissors; trims such as tulle netting, fabric scraps, and glitter; magnet strips; craft glue; pinch clothespins

Draw a ballerina shape on a piece of cardboard or poster board and cut it out. Decorate your figure. Cut out a piece of tulle or fabric to make a ballerina costume and glue it on the figure. Add glitter for her crown and toe shoes. Glue the ballerina to a pinch clothespin. Cut a piece of the magnet strip and glue it to the back of the clothespin. Use your clothespin magnet to hold your artwork on the refrigerator. Another idea is to decorate a clothespin magnet with Tiny Paper Flowers (see page 107).

CUSTOM CALENDAR 214

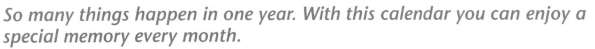

So many things happen in one year. With this calendar you can enjoy a special memory every month.

What You'll Need: 13 sheets of light-colored construction paper; hole punch; yarn; blunt scissors; coloring tools such as colored pencils, markers, or watercolor paints and paintbrush; craft glue (optional)

Set all 13 sheets of construction paper together. Punch 3 to 5 holes along one long edge. Thread a piece of yarn through the holes. Tie the ends together in a knot and trim any extra yarn. Punch 1 hole at the center of the opposite end. With the holes at the top, decorate the calendar cover.

Think about the types of activities your family or friends take part in each month. Draw a picture for each month, depicting these activities as well as the seasons. Use a different coloring tool for each month. To start, flip the first page. The page at the top (the back of the cover) is January. Decorate the page. Draw the actual calendar on the bottom sheet, copying from another calendar for the dates. Flip the page and do the same for February and the remaining months. Don't forget to write in special dates.

BAG PUPPETS

215

Create the characters from your favorite book and put on a show for your friends and family.

What You'll Need: Small lunch bags, markers, blunt scissors, pink and black felt, craft glue, brown buttons, black construction paper

You can make all kinds of puppets from bags. To get started, design a hound dog. Draw big spots on a bag. Use the crease of the bag for a mouth. Cut out a pink felt tongue and glue it on the bag. Glue 2 brown buttons for eyes. Add some fringed black construction paper for eyelashes. Cut 2 long ears from black felt. Glue an ear to each side of the bag. Put on a show, and have your puppet sing "Ain't Nothin' but a Hound Dog."

MATRIX GAME

216

This challenging puzzle game tests your strategic ability as well as your patience.

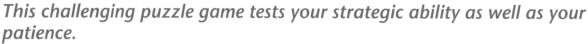

What You'll Need: 10×10-inch piece of poster board, 12×12-inch piece of poster board, ruler, markers, blunt scissors

Trace the outline of the small poster board on the large poster board. Draw a line every 2 inches on the small poster board up and down and across to make a matrix of 25 squares. There should be 5 squares down each side. Draw a picture on the small poster board, filling up all the squares except the one in the bottom right corner. Draw a small dot in the top left corner of each square. Cut out the squares. Throw away the blank bottom right square. Place the squares within the outline you drew on the large poster board. Mix the squares up, but keep all the dots in the top left corner. Re-create your picture by rearranging the squares one space and one square at a time.

CABLE CAR

217

Make a cable car to take your imagination to the top of a snow-covered mountain.

What You'll Need: Half-gallon milk or juice carton, scissors, permanent markers, string

Make a cable car from a half-gallon milk or juice carton. Ask an adult to cut out windows and a door for the cable car. Decorate your car with permanent markers. If you want, write the name of your cable car company on the carton. With an adult's help, poke 4 small holes at each corner of one side of the carton. Set up 2 chairs a short distance apart. Tie a long piece of string between the backs of the chairs in a loop. To make the cable cords, cut 4 pieces of string. Tie a knot at one end of each piece of string, and thread the string through each hole in the cable car. Tie the other end of the string to 1 line of the looped string. Pull the other side of the loop to make your cable car move between the chairs.

If you want to create a ski scene, throw a white blanket around one chair to make a mountain. Make little chalets and trees from small boxes and set them on the blankets. Make the Clothespin People on page 148, and give them a lift in the cable car.

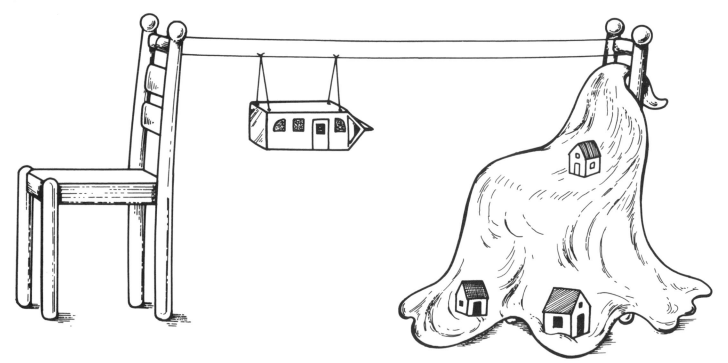

FLOPPY HORSESHOES

218

*Unlike most other games, in horseshoes you get points
when you hit the mark and even when you're close!*

What You'll Need: 8½×11-inch piece of cardboard, markers, ruler, blunt scissors, 1 yard foam sheet 1 inch thick (available at fabric stores), unsharpened pencil or drinking straw

On a piece of cardboard, draw a horseshoe 8 inches long, 7 inches wide, and 2 inches thick. Cut out the horseshoe pattern. Following the arrangement shown, trace six horseshoes on the foam sheet. Draw two 12-inch circles on the foam. Cut out the circles and horseshoes. Cut a tiny slit in the middle of each circle. Insert a thick drinking straw or an unsharpened pencil for the post. (You may need a little tape to help the post stand up straight.) If you want, decorate the circles and horseshoes with markers.

To play a game of horseshoes, you and a friend each get 3 horseshoes. Place the posts about 6 feet apart. Standing next to 1 post, throw your horseshoes at the opposite post. Take turns with your opponent throwing horseshoes at opposite posts. To score points, you get 3 points for a ringer (around the post) and 2 points for a leaner (touching the post). If no horseshoes touch the post, the person with the closest horseshoe gets 1 point. To make the game more challenging, move the posts 1 foot farther apart after each round. Keep track of your points—the first person to reach 50 points wins!

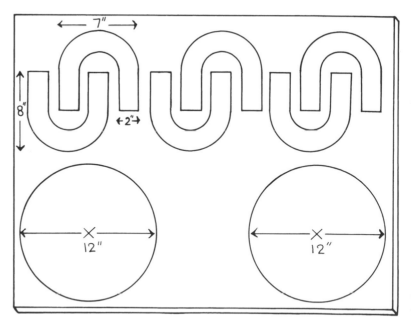

219 BRAINTEASER ART

Be sure to count your shapes as you draw the picture or you could end up teasing yourself.

What You'll Need: Paper, stencil shapes (available at office supply, craft, or art stores), pencil, markers

Use a stencil to create pictures out of geometric designs. Try a butterfly with lots of circles within circles or a house with squares for windows, shutters, chimneys, and even bricks. Keep track of the number of shapes you draw. If you want, use markers to make your brainteaser a kaleidoscope of color. When you're finished, challenge a friend or family member to count the shapes.

SPACE STATION 220

Someday, people might live and work in outer space. You can go there now in your imagination with this space station.

What You'll Need: Aluminum foil, boxes, clean foam food trays (from fruits or vegetables only), paper cups, scrap paper, transparent tape, craft glue, markers, scissors, string, oatmeal cartons, paper plates, paper tubes

Cover boxes, foam food trays, and paper cups with aluminum foil and white paper. Hold the foil and paper in place with tape or glue. Design a space insignia and draw it on some of the pieces. Have an adult cut out windows and landing pads. Tape all the pieces together to create a space station. Have an adult help you hang your space station with string in a doorway. Tape or glue foil around paper towel tubes, oatmeal cartons, and paper plates to make space shuttles and flying saucers. Have an adult cut out the bay doors, and add the wings, the tail, and the nose. Fly your spaceships in and out of the space station.

FRACTIONAL PIZZA GAME

221

These pizzas may not taste great, but the fun they serve up is absolutely delicious.

What You'll Need: Paper grocery bags, blunt scissors, markers, ruler, construction paper, paste, dice with fractions (see Giant Dice on page 126)

Cut 6 circles the same size from the grocery bags to make paper pizzas. On construction paper, draw your favorite pizza toppings such as pepperoni, mushrooms, sausage, and tomatoes. Cut the toppings out and paste them on the paper pizzas. With a marker, divide your pizzas into these fractions: ½, ⅓, ¼, ⅙, ⅛, and 1/12, and cut the "slices." (You may need an adult's help to make sure your slices are even.) See Giant Dice on page 126 to make a die with fractions on its 6 sides. To play the game, roll the die and select the slice size it shows. The first person to assemble a whole pizza wins!

MAILING TUBE

222

Imagine the expressions on your friends' faces when they receive mail in a tube!

What You'll Need: Wrapping paper tube, markers, white mailing labels, pencil, thin cardboard, blunt scissors, packing tape

To make a mailing tube, decorate the cardboard tube from a roll of wrapping paper. Use markers to color it in a wild and colorful pattern. Stick a white mailing label on the tube for the sender's address. Add another label for your return address. To make the end caps, trace the end of the roll on the cardboard twice. Cut both circles out. Tape 1 circle securely to one end of the mailing tube. Roll up the letter or artwork you are sending and insert it into the tube. See the Self-Portraits project on page 100 to send a picture of yourself. Tape the other end cap to the open end of the tube.

POP-UP GREETING CARD

223

Give a little extra lift to your message with a special greeting card that springs to life.

What You'll Need: Construction paper, ruler, pencil, blunt scissors, craft glue, markers

1. Fold a piece of construction paper in half. Halfway down the fold, make 2 pencil marks about 2 inches apart. At each mark, cut a slit through the fold 1 inch into the paper.

2. Fold the cut flap back and forth several times to crease it well. Bring the flap back to center. Unfold the page almost completely, and gently push the flap through to the other side. You should have a rectangle that pops out of the paper.

3. Draw a shape or design for your greeting card on another piece of construction paper. Cut it out, and glue it to the front of the pop-out rectangle. Fold another piece of construction paper in half. Trim the pop-up paper so that it is slightly smaller than the second piece of paper. Glue the back of the pop-up paper to the inside of the larger paper. Decorate the front of your greeting card, and write a message inside.

4. If you want to make your pop-up cards into a pop-up gift book, repeat steps 1 and 2 to make several pop-up pages. Then draw and cut out the items for your story from construction paper. Glue those shapes on the pop-out rectangles. Glue the back of one page to the front of another. Repeat this until all the pages are glued together. To make a cover, fold another piece of construction paper in half. Glue the first and last pages inside the cover. Decorate the cover of your book.

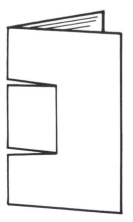

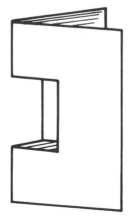

MARIONETTE PUPPET

224

With a little practice, you and a friend can perform your very own puppet show with marionettes.

What You'll Need: One 1×2-inch board about 5 inches long (for the body), four 4½-inch wood dowels with ½-inch diameter (for the arms and legs), two 12-inch wood dowels with ½-inch diameter (for the control bars), one 2-inch wood dowel with ½-inch diameter (for the neck), saw, sandpaper, power drill with ½-inch and ⅛-inch drill bits, fishing line or string, blunt scissors, wood glue, one 2-inch wood bead (for the head), markers

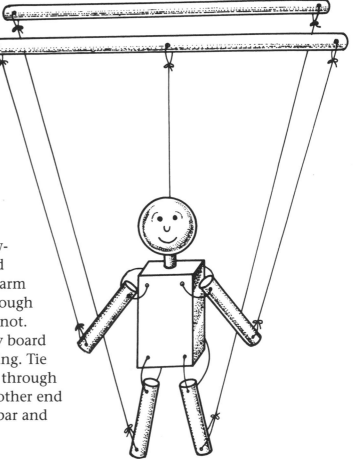

Preparing the wood pieces: Since this project involves drilling and sawing, you'll need an adult to help you. Start by helping mom or dad cut and sand all the wood pieces. Then have an adult drill all the holes in the wood pieces. To make the marionette body, drill a ⅛-inch hole in each corner of the 1×2-inch board all the way through the wood. Drill ⅛-inch holes in each end of the arm and leg dowels. Then drill ⅛-inch holes in each end of the control bars. Drill another hole in the middle of one bar. Switch drill bits and drill a ½-inch hole in the short end of the body board.

Attaching the parts: Cut 4 short pieces of fishing line or string. Tie the arms and legs to the body following the illustration. Cut 4 long pieces of string. Thread one end of each string through the end holes of each arm and leg and tie it in a knot. Thread the other ends through corresponding holes on the control bars and tie in a knot. Glue the 2-inch dowel in the ½-inch hole on the body board for the neck. Let the glue set. Cut another piece of string. Tie one end around the end of the neck. Thread the bead through the string, and glue the bead to the neck. Thread the other end of the string through the middle hole on the control bar and tie it in a knot. Draw a face on the wood bead.

225 FLIP BALL PADDLE

Challenge your hand-eye coordination with this easy-to-make paddle game.

What You'll Need: Paper plate, markers, blunt scissors, paint stirring stick, craft glue, hole punch, small ball, netted fruit bag, string

Draw a fun character's face on the paper plate. Cut out the eyes and mouth. Make sure the holes are slightly bigger than the ball. Glue the paint stirring stick to the back of the plate. Punch a small hole in the plate just below the mouth. Cut a piece of netting from the fruit bag large enough to cover the ball. Wrap the ball in the netting and tie it closed with one end of the string. Tie the other end of the string through the small hole in the plate. Try to flip the ball through the holes.

FANCY BOA 226

A boa is a glamourous accessory. Here's one you can make the next time you play dress up.

What You'll Need: Plastic needlepoint needle, measuring tape, 2 yards of tulle netting, yarn, blunt scissors, glitter or sequins and craft glue (optional)

Thread the needle with about 4 feet of yarn. Tie a knot at one end. Cut all the netting into 4-inch-wide strips. Use the needle and yarn to sew a gathering stitch through the netting. Thread the yarn in and out in even stitches about 1 inch apart down the center of the netting. Every yard or so, bunch up the netting. Continue stitching onto another strip until you have used all the netting strips. Trim off the excess yarn, and tie it in a knot. Spread the netting out evenly. If you want to add sparkle to your boa, glue on glitter or sequins.

CLOTHESPIN PEOPLE

227

Create your own action figures—family members, super heroes, or even an Olympic ski team!

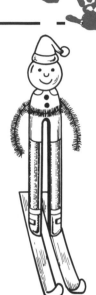

What You'll Need: Newspaper, slotted round wooden clothespin, acrylic paints and paintbrush, fine-point markers, pipe cleaner, craft glue, felt scraps, construction paper

Cover your work surface with newspaper. Paint on clothes for your clothespin person, letting the paint dry between each section. Paint the bottom ½ inch for the shoes. Paint the slotted "legs" for the pants. Paint the top part of the clothespin body for the shirt. (Leave the knob unpainted.) Draw a face on the knob of the clothespin using fine-point markers. To make the arms, wrap a pipe cleaner around the middle of the shirt and glue it in place. Cut a hat from felt, and glue it on top of the head. Cut small paper skis, and glue them to the bottom of the clothespin legs.

BASEBALL TARGET GAME

228

No more rained out games. Now you can play baseball in the house with this indoor target game.

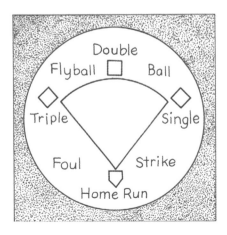

Double
Flyball ☐ Ball
Triple ◇ ◇ Single
Foul Strike
Home Run

What You'll Need: 12 inches of ½-inch-wide hook-and-loop tape (hook part), ruler, blunt scissors, 4 table tennis balls, fabric glue, 16×18-inch piece of light-colored felt, 2 pieces of cardboard (one 16×18-inch piece and one 4×6-inch piece), permanent markers

Cut the hook-and-loop tape into four 2-inch pieces. Glue a piece around each table tennis ball. Glue the felt on the large cardboard piece. Let the glue set. Draw a baseball diamond on the felt, and label it as shown. Cut 4 baseball players about 1-inch wide from the small cardboard piece. Glue a square of hook-and-loop tape to the back of each player. Place the players on the baseball diamond to keep track of balls, strikes, outs, and runs scored.

GAME PIECES

229

Design custom game pieces for your family and friends, or replace missing pieces from your favorite board game.

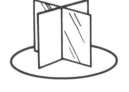

What You'll Need: Craft foam (available at craft stores), blunt scissors, permanent markers, craft glue

Cut 2 identical shapes from the foam. Cut geometric shapes such as a square, circle, or hexagon to replace missing pieces from a board game, or customize the pieces for your family or friends. On both pieces, draw the features of a friend or family member—same color eyes, hair, and so on. Add earrings, a hat, or any other feature that represents that person.

In the top of one shape and the bottom of the other, cut a slit about ½ of the length of the shape. Fit the shapes together. Cut a circle about the same size as the shapes from the foam. Glue the circular base to the game piece. Let the glue dry.

FOAM CORE PUZZLE

230

To make your puzzle even more challenging, use a picture with only a few colors.

What You'll Need: Magazine picture, photograph, or artwork, foam core board or plastic foam picnic plates, craft glue, craft knife

Ask an adult to help you with this project. Select a picture from a magazine, a large photograph, or your own artwork. Glue the picture to the foam core board or picnic plate. Cut out the picture in a square or circle with a small border for edge pieces. Have an adult help you cut your picture into curvy and zigzag pieces with a craft knife. Now mix the pieces up and try to put the picture back together.

CHECKERS

231

A game of checkers is even more fun when you design the pieces yourself!

What You'll Need: Waxed paper, white polymer clay, rolling pin, cap from a plastic milk jug or water bottle, a quarter, acrylic paints, paintbrush, ruler, black felt-tip pen, a large, clean pizza box

Cover your work surface with a sheet of waxed paper. Roll out a sheet of white polymer clay, about ½ inch thick. Use the milk jug or water bottle cap to press out 24 circles. Press a design on each circle using a quarter. With an adult's help, bake the clay checker pieces following the package directions. After the clay pieces have cooled, paint 12 pieces one color and the other 12 pieces a different color. Let the paint dry.

To make the checkerboard pattern, draw a 16×16-inch square inside the pizza box. Draw lines to make 64 squares, 2 inches each. Start by drawing a line down the center of the square and another line across the center of the square. This divides each side of the square in half. Now draw lines to divide each of those squares in half. Then draw more lines to divide each of those squares half. There should be 8 squares down each side. Paint every square to finish the checkerboard pattern. If you want, paint the outside of the box, too. Let the paint dry. Line up the opposing game pieces on each side of the board to play a game of checkers. Store your checker pieces inside the box when you are done.

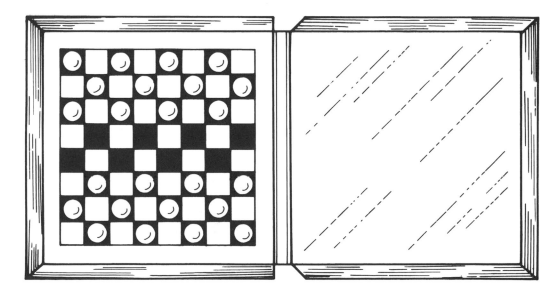

TWIST-TIE PICKUPS

232

Get hooked on this fun game. But be careful—one wrong move and your chain falls apart.

What You'll Need: Large piece thin poster board, blunt scissors, markers, twist ties (about 40), craft glue

On the poster board, draw a figure with a head and body. Cut it out and trace it 19 times on the remaining poster board. Cut out all the figures and decorate them. Glue 2 figures back to back with twist ties between the pieces for legs and arms. Make 9 more two-sided figures the same way. Let the glue set.

Bend the arms and legs in different directions to make hooks. To play the game, hold one figure and try to pick up another by hooking it to the first. Holding only the first figure, hook another figure to the second figure. See how many figures you can pick up before the chain breaks.

ART FLASH CARDS

233

Teach yourself to see basic shapes in your art with a fun flash card game.

What You'll Need: Ten 3×5-inch blank index cards, markers

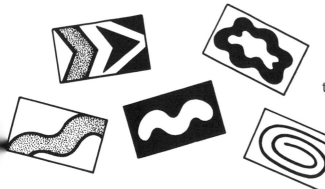

Divide the index cards between you and a friend. Draw crazy shapes on the cards. Start with simple shapes without too many intersecting lines, then make each shape a little more complicated. Don't draw letters or specific objects. The idea is to draw unfamiliar shapes. Color in the shapes. Now flash one card at a time to each other. See if you and your friend can redraw the shape you were shown. Hold the picture at different angles and distances. Can you see any objects in your art?

TODDLER CAN

234

Make an educational toy for a little girl or boy in your family. They'll get hours of pleasure from your gift.

What You'll Need: Empty coffee can, can opener, blunt scissors, assorted colors of felt, craft glue, fabric markers, 3 plastic coffee can lids, clothespins, blocks, large poker chips

With an adult's help, use a can opener to cut the tin lid and bottom from a coffee can. Cut a piece of felt to fit around the can. Cut the width about 1 inch wider than the can. Glue the felt around the coffee can. Fold and glue the 1-inch excess over the bottom edge of the can to cover rough edges. Decorate the felt with cut felt shapes and fabric markers. Have an adult cut in each lid: a circle to fit clothespins, a square to fit blocks, and a slit to fit large poker chips. (You can also cut a circle, square, and slit in one lid to make a shape-sorter toy.) To play, put a lid on the can and place it on a flat surface. Have the toddler put the shapes in the can.

PASTA JEWELRY

235

Be a trendsetter with this fashion "Italian" jewelry. It's the perfect touch to any outfit.

What You'll Need: Waxed paper, assorted pasta shapes with holes, poster paints, paintbrush, yarn, craft glue and construction paper (optional)

Cover your work surface with waxed paper. Color several pasta pieces with poster paints. (The amount depends on the length of the necklace you want to make.) Paint stripes, polka dots, or solid colors on the pasta "beads." Let them dry. Then string the "beads" on a piece of yarn. Tie the ends together in a knot. Make bracelets to match your necklaces. To make a ring, glue 1 pasta piece on a band of paper.

PUPPETS WITH LEGS

236

With the help of your fingers, these puppets come alive and dance across the stage.

What You'll Need: Poster board, markers, blunt scissors, trims such as feathers, yarn, or felt scraps, craft glue

On a piece of poster board, draw an animal or person from the thighs up. For example, draw a bird's head, body, wings, and tail for the puppet shape. Use markers to color in the details. Cut out the puppet shape. Cut two holes at the bottom of the shape. Make sure they are large enough for your middle and index fingers since your fingers will be the bird's legs. Glue on trims such as feathers to decorate your bird. Put your fingers through the holes and make your bird puppet dance. Make more puppets to put on a show with your friends.

CAR RACE GAME

237

Draw your own grand prix track and race a friend to the finish line.

What You'll Need: Graph paper, markers, die

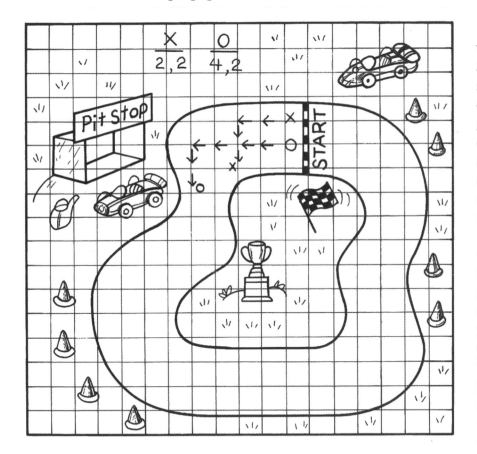

Draw a curvy track at least 1 inch wide on a piece of graph paper. Draw a tiny grandstand, start/finish line, pit stop area, and walls. To make your "race cars," cut 2 squares from another piece of graph paper the same size as the squares on the graph paper track. Mark one with an X and one with an O. Or instead of an X and O, you can draw one type of car on a square and a different car on the other square.

To play the game: Place your cars at the start line. Roll the die to determine how many squares to move. You may move your car in only one direction—either across or down. You may not move diagonally. If your move sends your car off the track, you lose a turn. When it's your turn again, you come back to the last spot you were on inside the track. If you land on the same spot as the other car, go back to the last spot you were on and skip a turn. Take turns with your friend moving your race cars. The first one to cross the finish line wins.

DESIGN A MENU

238

Imagine a restaurant that serves silly food. Then invent a fun menu for your new restaurant.

What You'll Need: Construction paper, markers, black felt-tip pen

Design a menu for a specialty restaurant. Make it silly with chicken everything—soup, chicken desserts, and even chicken drinks. Fold a large piece of construction paper in half lengthwise. Write your items on the menu, and decorate it to match your restaurant theme. You can even add outrageous prices for your silly dishes.

If you don't want a silly menu, make a real one with your favorite dishes. Use a grocery store circular to cut and paste food pictures on the menu. Play a game of restaurant with your friends. Gather some play dishes, a tray, and an apron. Draw order forms on a piece of paper. Give your friends a menu and take their orders.

SOAP SCULPTURES

239

Turn routine hand washing into an amusing game with these delightful little soap sculptures.

What You'll Need: Soap flakes, medium-size bowl, spoon, water, food coloring, scented oil (optional), waxed paper

Pour some soap flakes in a medium-size bowl. Gradually stir in water until the mixture reaches a stiff, doughlike consistency. Add a few drops of food coloring to the mixture to make colored soaps. If you want to make scented soaps, add a few drops of scented oil to the batch. Cover your work surface with waxed paper. Place the dough on the waxed paper, and sculpt it into shapes such as shells, butterflies, or hearts. Let them dry overnight. Place them in a gift box (see Chinese Gift Cartons on page 129), and give them to your friends or family members.

NO-SEW DOLL FASHIONS

240

Pretend you're a world famous fashion designer and create a new wardrobe for your dolls or stuffed animals.

What You'll Need: Materials such as old socks and ties, blunt scissors, trims such as ribbon or sequins, craft glue

You can make all kinds of cool fashions for your dolls with materials such as old socks and ties. Here are a few ideas to get you started. Cut the toe area out from a sock. Cut holes for the neck and arms in the end of the toe for a blouse. Cut the ankle area out from the same sock. Tie ribbon around one end to make a gathered waist for a skirt. Decorate your skirt and blouse with trims such as ribbon or sequins. If you want to add a shawl, cut a strip from the middle of an old tie.

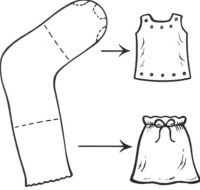

PARENT'S JOB LIST

241

This clever little book shows mom and dad how much you appreciate everything you do for you.

What You'll Need: Notebook or typing paper, pencil, construction paper, markers, craft glue, blunt scissors

Write a list of all the jobs your mom or dad does for the family. In addition to obvious jobs such as cook and driver, think creatively and list jobs such as banker and decorator. After you've compiled your list, draw on a piece of construction paper your parents performing each job. Make your pictures into a book. Glue your pictures in a heart-shaped book you make yourself (see Book of Promises on page 159), or bind your drawings in a scrapbook (see Scrapbook Binding on page 89). Give the book to your parent for Mother's or Father's Day.

CODE WHEEL

242

You and a friend can pretend you're secret agents and send each other important messages in code.

What You'll Need: Poster board or 2 small paper plates, blunt scissors, ruler or compass, pencil, brass paper fastener, ballpoint pen

Cut 2 circles, 6 inches each from posterboard. (You can also use 2 small paper plates.) Cut a ½-inch-wide V-shape and a ½-inch-round window in one circle wheel as shown. Use the pencil to poke a small hole in the center of both wheels. Attach the wheels with a brass paper fastener. Write the letter *A* in the V, then turn the wheel ½ inch and write the letter *B*. Continue with the rest of the alphabet around the wheel. (Hint: You can measure ½ inch without a ruler. Make a small pencil mark on the right side of the V, then turn the wheel so the left side lines up with the mark.)

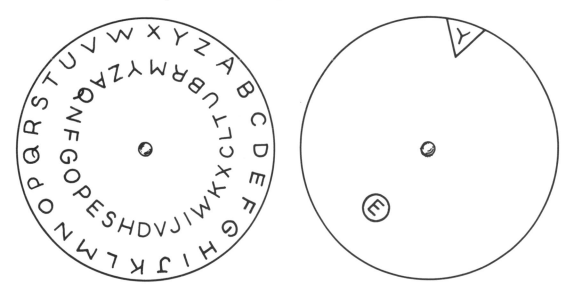

Now fill in the window. Turn the wheel. Write the letter *A* in the window. (Make sure the V is not pointing to the letter *A*!) Turn the wheel several inches and write a *B* in the window. Place the rest of the alphabet in the window, always making sure the window letter is different than the V letter. Make a second wheel for your friend that matches yours exactly so you can write and decode secret messages.

243

SOCK PUPPETS

Make a cast of colorful characters with old socks in bright colors.

What You'll Need: Old, clean sock, needle and thread, blunt scissors, 2 buttons, fabric markers, felt, fabric glue

Make a dragon sock puppet. With an adult's help, sew on button eyes to your sock. Be sure you don't sew through to the other side. Draw 2 eyelash shapes on a piece of felt and cut them out. Glue the eyelashes to the sock above the button eyes. Draw a mouth and scales on the dragon with markers. Draw and cut out the dragon's tongue, wings, and spikes from the felt. Refer to the illustration, and glue the pieces to the dragon. Make more puppets with other socks. Add trims to make a princess and a knight. Use felt pieces for their clothes and features and yarn for their hair. Now you're ready to put on a puppet show. See Puppet Theater on page 137 or Big Box Bonanza on page 76 to make a stage.

BOOK OF PROMISES

244

Sometimes the best gift doesn't cost a penny. Give a promise worth a million bucks to mom or dad.

What You'll Need: Construction paper, blunt scissors, typing paper, pencil, stapler and staples, markers or colored pencils

To make a cover for your book, fold a piece of construction paper in half. Draw a heart as shown, and cut it out. Fold 3 pieces of typing paper together. Trace the heart on the top, and cut it out. Insert the pages in the cover and staple the spine. Write a promise on each page—they can be serious or silly. Decorate the pages with pictures to illustrate your promise.

I promise to help with the dishes

PAINT-A-GIFT

245

Grown-ups like presents as much as kids, and they especially like gifts hand made by you!

What You'll Need: Newspaper, plain apron, large piece of cardboard, straight pins or binder clips, small dish, acrylic paints, paintbrush

Cover your work surface with newspaper. Pin or clip the apron to the cardboard to hold it in place as you paint it. Place some water in a small dish. Paint a design around the edges of the apron with slightly thinned acrylic paints. As you paint, dip the paintbrush in water, then dip the brush in the paint to thin it. Paint cooking utensils for a dad who likes to barbecue or flowers for a mom who likes gardening. If you want, use stencils to make a design. (See Stencil Art on page 87.) Let the paint dry, then wrap your gift.

YEAR-ROUND CRAFTS

You can enjoy arts and crafts all year—for holidays, birthdays, family celebrations, warm days, and even stay-inside days. This chapter starts with activities for parties and all seasons. As you continue through the chapter, you'll find projects for winter, spring, summer, and fall. While most of the projects have a particular product for a specific time of the year, you can still turn one season's idea into another season's fun. Dying Easter eggs is a process that is fun in the spring, but it can also be adapted as a fall activity to make Thanksgiving eggs. With a little imagination, there's something here for everyone at any time of the year.

NAPKIN RINGS

Coordinate these napkin rings with other table decorations to create a table setting with a theme.

What You'll Need: Construction paper, blunt scissors, paper towel tubes, craft glue, markers

Cut construction paper to fit around a paper towel tube. Glue the paper around the tube. Repeat with other paper towel tubes using different colors of paper. Cut the paper towel tubes into 2-inch rings. Use markers and cutout shapes to decorate each napkin ring. Write each guest's name on a napkin ring to make place cards. Cut out circles or other shapes from construction paper and glue them to the napkin rings. For birthday parties, make the ring look like a cake. For a picnic, decorate the rings with red and white checkerboards to look like the napkins. For an everyday dinner, draw on something that each family member likes to eat.

BOX MAZE

247

Make two box mazes and have races with a friend. If you can finish without losing your marbles, you win.

What You'll Need: Drawing paper, pencil, scissors, markers, small marble, shoe box with lid, craft glue

Have an adult help you with the cutting. Practice drawing a maze design on a piece of paper. Think of a theme for your maze. For example, it might be a swamp game such as "Watch Out for the Alligator Ponds." Draw lines for the maze walls, and mark places along the maze to cut holes (the ponds) for the marble to fall through. Mark the starting and finishing points of the maze. Once you've created a design you like, draw the maze lines and hole marks on the inside of the shoe box lid. Cut the pond holes where indicated. Make sure the holes are slightly larger than the marble. Decorate the maze with markers. To make the maze walls, cut ½-inch-wide strips of cardboard from the rest of the shoe box. The strips should be the length of each maze line. Apply glue along the lines in the lid, and stand a cardboard strip in the glue to make each wall. Let the glue dry. To play, place a marble at the starting point. Then tilt and turn the lid to move the marble along the maze to the finishing point. Be sure to watch out for the alligator pond holes!

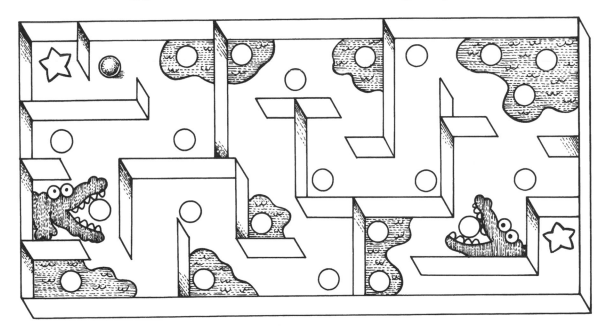

CURLY PAPER ART

248

You can make just about anything with curly paper, but it looks especially elegant hanging on a Christmas tree.

What You'll Need: Construction paper, blunt scissors, transparent tape

To make a curly paper ornament, cut 2 long strips and 2 short strips of construction paper. Tape the 2 long and 2 short strips together at the top and bottom. Separate the strips at one end. Cut 2 more short strips. Tape the ends together to form rings. Tape the rings between the long strips. Fanfold some more short strips and tape them in between. Cut 4 strips and curl them over the edge of a closed pair of scissors. Tape the curly strips to the bottom. Make a loop with a short strip of paper and tape it to the top of the ornament to hang it.

BAND: SAND BLOCKS

249

This one percussion instrument produces two very different sounds—one by tapping the blocks and another by scraping the blocks.

What You'll Need: Two 2×3-inch wood blocks at least 5 inches long, two 2×2-inch wood blocks at least 2 inches long, saw, blunt scissors, sandpaper, wood glue, rubber bands

Ask an adult to help you cut the wood pieces. Cut each 2×3-inch block to 5 inches. Cut the 2×2-inch blocks to 2 inches. (If you have an old block set, you can use 2 large and 2 small blocks.) Cut the sandpaper to fit around the bottom and sides of the large block. Wrap the sandpaper around the large block and glue it in place. Place a rubber band around each end to hold the sandpaper in place as the glue dries. To make the handle, glue a small block on top of the large block. Let the glue dry overnight. Make another sand block with the remaining wood pieces.

BAND: JINGLE BELLS

250

Turn your body into a musical instrument with jingle bells you can wear as a bracelet.

What You'll Need: 16 inches of grosgrain ribbon or bias tape, 6 jingle bells, blunt scissors, needle and thread, 2 sets of snaps

Cut the ribbon or bias tape in half. Sew on 3 jingle bells, evenly spaced apart, on 1 piece of ribbon or bias tape. Sew a snap on each end. Snap the ends together around your wrist to form a jingle bell bracelet. Use the other piece of ribbon to make a second bracelet. Once you put the bracelets on, shake your arms to make some music. If you want, make jingle bell bracelets for your ankles, too. Listen to them jingle when you march with the band.

BAND: DRUM

251

Use your bongo drum to create different sounds with your fingertips or the palm and heel of your hand.

What You'll Need: Oatmeal carton, construction paper, blunt scissors, markers, craft glue, ribbon

Cut a piece of construction paper to fit around an oatmeal carton. Draw a picture of palm trees on the paper for a Caribbean design. Wrap the paper around the oatmeal carton with the design facing out. Glue it in place. To make a strap, have an adult poke a hole in each side of the carton near the top. Remove the lid. Cut a long piece of ribbon. Thread the ends through each hole and tie a double knot in each end. Put the lid back on the carton. Place the strap over your shoulders and march around while you beat a rhythm on the lid.

BAND: MARACAS

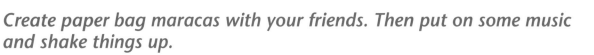

252

Create paper bag maracas with your friends. Then put on some music and shake things up.

What You'll Need: Newspaper, small paper bags or bakery bags, poster paints, paintbrush, dried beans, small pebbles, or seeds, craft glue

Cover your work surface with newspaper. Decorate the outside of 2 paper bags with poster paints. Paint stripes, zigzags, or a Caribbean design to match your other band instruments. After the paint has dried, put dried beans, small pebbles, or seeds in the bags. Thin the craft glue with 2 teaspoons of water. Paint the outside of the bags with the diluted glue. While the glue is still wet, twist the top 4 inches of each bag into a handle. Coat the handles with another layer of glue. Let it dry overnight.

NEWSPAPER HATS

253

Gather lots of hat-making supplies, and let everyone at your birthday party make their own newspaper cap.

What You'll Need: Newspaper, transparent tape, trims such as pom-poms or tissue paper fringe (optional)

1. To make a basic newspaper hat, fold 1 newspaper page in half horizontally. (If you want to make a large hat, use 2 newspaper pages, and fold it in half vertically.) With the fold at the top, fold the top corners in to the center. Tape the points down.

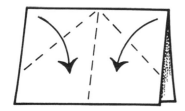

Fold the top corners to the center.

2. Fold up the bottom edges.

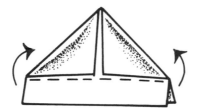

Fold up the bottom edges.

3. Tuck in the corner edges and add tape to hold them in place. If you want, trim your hat with pom-poms or tissue paper fringe. Put your hat on and wear it with the points at the front and back or to the side.

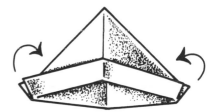

Tuck in corners.

PARROT PIÑATA

254

A piñata is a decorated container filled with sweet treats. You hit the piñata and when it bursts, everyone gathers the goodies.

What You'll Need: Newspaper, large (12-inch) balloon, flour and water (for paste), measuring cup, ruler, blunt scissors, poster paints, paintbrush, markers, poster board, masking tape, colored tissue paper, craft glue, assorted candy, strong string

1. Cover your work surface with newspaper. Blow up the balloon and knot the end. Mix flour and water together to make a paste. Use 1 cup of flour for each cup of water. Blend until the paste is smooth. Cut 7 or 8 pages of newspaper into 1×4-inch strips. Dip a strip of newspaper in the paste. Rub the strip between your fingers to remove any extra paste. Place the strip over the balloon and smooth in place. Continue covering the whole balloon with a layer of strips, overlapping them slightly. Then apply 3 more layers of strips. Let the balloon dry for a few days. Once dry, carefully poke 2 small holes at the top about 4 inches apart.

Cover balloon with strips.

2. Paint the balloon body in bright colors. Let the paint dry. Draw a parrot head shape and 2 wing shapes on a piece of poster board. Color them in or add detail with markers. Cut the shapes from poster board and tape them to the balloon body. Dab paint over the tape to conceal it. Cut long strips of colored tissue paper for the parrot's tail. Glue the tissue paper strips to the balloon body.

Cut out parrot head and wings.

3. With an adult's help, cut a 3-inch-wide triangular flap between the 2 top holes. Fold down the flap to remove the balloon and fill the piñata with candy. To make the hanger, thread a piece of string through the 2 top holes and knot the ends. Push the flap back in place.

Cut a triangular flap to fill the piñata with candy.

FOOT DRAWING

It's hard to say which is more fun: trying to master foot drawing yourself or watching someone else try it.

What You'll Need: Large pieces of paper, markers

Foot drawing makes a great party project. Have everyone sit in a chair, and place a large piece of paper by the foot of each chair. Give everyone a marker to draw with. Don't let them hold the marker in their hands—instead they have to hold the marker between their toes! Now everyone can start drawing. Have them start by trying to write their name, then have them draw a picture. When everyone's done, compare their foot drawings. Save the drawings as souvenirs from your party.

PERSONALIZED PARTY PLATES

Make all your party guests feel like the guest of honor with these personalized plates.

What You'll Need: Paper plates, markers, clear plastic wrap, blunt scissors, craft glue

Draw a special picture on each paper plate for your guests. If you want to use the plates as place cards, write each guest's name on it. For each plate, cut a circle of clear plastic wrap the same size as the plate. Apply a ring of glue around the rim of 1 plate. Add a dot of glue to the center of the plate. Cover the plate with a circle of plastic wrap to seal your picture. Repeat for the remaining plates. You can use these plates to serve anything that doesn't need to be cut with a knife. Ice cream and cake, cookies, or cheese and crackers all work just fine.

HOLIDAY FANFOLDS

257

Here are several ways a folded fan can add three-dimensional interest to a flat picture.

What You'll Need: Construction paper, blunt scissors, ruler, transparent tape, markers

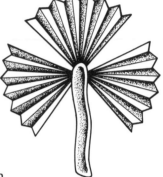

Cut a 3×6-inch rectangle from a piece of construction paper. Fold the short edge back ½ inch. Turn the paper over and fold the fold back the same distance. Repeat until the whole paper is folded. Pinch one end together to make a fan triangle and tape the end to secure it.

Here are just a few holiday projects you can make with fanfolds. Decorate a fan triangle with markers to make a Christmas tree. Make 2 triangles and use them for angel or bird wings. Tape a fan triangle on a turkey cutout for a tail. Make 3 triangles for a shamrock. Instead of a bow, use 2 triangles on a present.

SPONGE AROUND PRINTING

258

This painting technique produces artwork in seconds. It's a handy trick if you need to make a lot of party invitations.

What You'll Need: Old magazines, blunt scissors, pencil, poster board, sponges, newspaper, construction paper, poster paints, markers

Cut out a holiday picture from a magazine. Choose a simple outline of Santa, the Easter bunny, or a Halloween pumpkin. Trace around your picture on poster board and then cut it out. Cover your work surface with newspaper. Dip a damp sponge in some poster paint. Dab the excess on a scrap piece of paper. Place the cutout on a piece of construction paper and sponge around it with the paint. When the paint is dry, use a marker to write a holiday greeting or party information inside the paint outline.

THUMMIES

With your thumbprint as a starting point, you can come up with all sorts of art creations.

What You'll Need: Water-based ink stamp pad, drawing paper, fine-point felt-tip pen

Press your thumb on an ink pad, then press it on a piece of paper. With a fine-point felt-tip pen, add details to your thumbprint to create an animal, a person, or a silly character. Draw ears, whiskers, and a tail to make a cat, or add spots, legs, and antennas to make a ladybug. There are so many fun creations you can make with thummies. Try using your pinky or index finger for prints in different sizes and shapes. Or press 4 or 5 thummies in a row to make a caterpillar. Use thummies to decorate greeting cards and stationery or to illustrate a story.

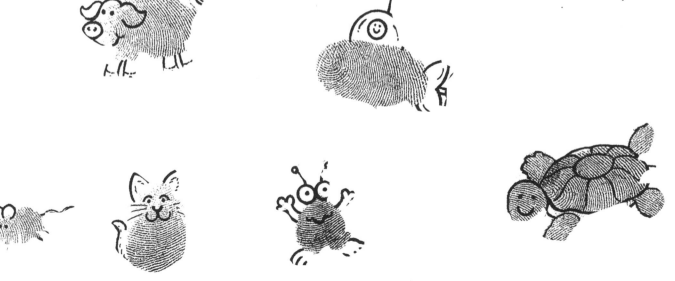

THANK YOUS

260

When someone brings you an extra special present, say "thank you" in an equally special way.

What You'll Need: Construction paper, markers

Make a picture card to thank someone for a birthday or holiday present. Fold a piece of construction paper in half. Write the words *thank you* on the front. Make one letter in *thank you* into a picture of the gift you received. If you received a doll, then draw a doll with her arms up for the letter *y*. Write the rest of the letters in colorful markers. You can also make birthday, congratulations, and get well soon cards with pictures as the letters. Draw birthday candles to make some letters in *Happy Birthday,* or make the word *soon* into a sickbed for a get well card.

SEE-THROUGH PICTURE

When the sun shines through these see-through pictures, the colors become bolder and brighter.

What You'll Need: Construction paper, blunt scissors, transparent tape, clear plastic wrap, permanent markers

Fold a piece of construction paper in half, then fold it in half again. Cut out a square on each fold. Unfold the paper and tape a piece of plastic wrap behind the cutout holes. Draw pictures on the plastic wrap with permanent markers. Add dark outlines to bright colors. Use see-through pictures to make holiday decorations for your front window.

DOORKNOB HANGERS

These doorknob hangers have a notepad so you can leave notes for your family all year-round.

Went to the pool.

What You'll Need: Poster board, pencil, ruler, blunt scissors, markers, self-stick removable notes, construction paper, craft glue

Make a doorknob hanger for each season. Refer to the illustration to draw a 4×8-inch doorknob hanger pattern on a piece of poster board. Cut the pattern out and trace it 3 times on the poster board. Cut out each piece. You should have 4 doorknob hangers. Decorate each one to match a season. A summer hanger might have a sprig of flowers with summer bugs crawling up it or children diving into a pool. Leave a space toward the bottom for the notepad. For the notepad, place the self-stick removable notes on the doorknob hanger. Cut a strip of construction paper to make a pencil holder loop. Glue it to the side of the notepad.

263 GLITTER ORNAMENTS

With a little glue and glitter, you can make a shimmering ornament for each member of your family.

What You'll Need: Waxed paper, craft glue, assorted colors of glitter, thread

Draw an ornament design on a sheet of waxed paper with a thick line of white glue. If you can't think of a shape, put a simple picture under the waxed paper and trace it with the glue. Shake glitter over the glue, covering the glue completely. Let it set overnight. The next day, shake off the excess glitter. Peel the waxed paper off and tie on a piece of thread for the hanger. Make a set of ornaments for your family. Make something that each member of your family uses in his or her hobby such as in-line skates or a flower.

HOLIDAY MOBILE 264

Let the wind spin and twirl your mobile. It's a great way to see your project from every angle.

What You'll Need: Plastic coffee can lid, scissors, permanent markers, hole punch, string

To make the frame, have an adult cut the center from a plastic coffee can lid. Make sure the rim is at least ½ inch wide. Color the rim with permanent markers. To make the hanger, punch 4 holes evenly spaced around the rim. Thread a piece of string through each hole. Bring the ends of each string together at the top and tie them in a knot. Punch 4 more holes between the others. Hang string down from the 4 holes to hold your decorations. Each season of the year, tie on something new: Christmas ornaments, paper Easter eggs, or Halloween ghosts and goblins.

YEAR-ROUND WREATH

265

Who says wreaths are only for Christmas? Challenge yourself to design a wreath for each month of the year.

What You'll Need: 2 brown paper grocery bags, blunt scissors, transparent tape, craft glue, ribbon, construction paper, removable tape

1. Cut off the bottom of a grocery bag, and cut a seam down one side to make a large sheet. Repeat with the other bag.

2. Place the bags on top of each other and tape them together. Roll the bags to make a long log. Twist the bags slightly as you roll them together.

3. Tape the two ends together, forming a circle. This is the wreath base. Tie a piece of ribbon into a bow, and glue it over the ends of the wreath. Decorate the wreath with paper cutouts for each month. From construction paper, cut out January snowflakes, February hearts, March shamrocks, and so on. Attach the cutouts to the wreath using removable tape. Change the cutouts each month.

Roll two grocery bags together.

Cut a grocery bag.

Tape ends together forming a circle.

BASKETS & BOXES

266

These boxes and baskets hold all sorts of lightweight holiday treats for Easter, Christmas, or birthday parties.

What You'll Need: Poster board, pencil, ruler, blunt scissors, markers, stapler and staples

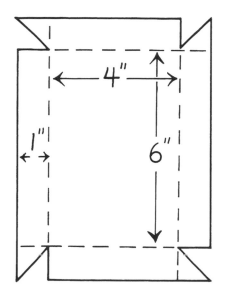

Copy the pattern shown on a piece of poster board. Use a ruler to measure the base and sides. Cut the pattern out. Use markers to decorate your box before you fold it. Draw a design on the sides that will be facing out. Score along the dotted lines. (See Advanced Paper Folding on page 78 for the scoring technique.) Fold the poster board on the scored lines and staple it into a box. To make a handle for a basket, cut a 2×7-inch strip of poster board. Staple across the top of the box. To make a lid for a box, make another box slightly larger than the first, adding about ⅜ inch to the rectangle on each side. Place the lid on the box.

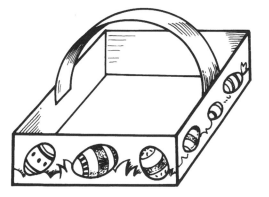

267 FOUR SEASONS TREE

Don't wait for the next holiday—celebrate now with a tree for all seasons.

What You'll Need: Thin tree branches or twigs, construction paper, blunt scissors, markers or colored pencils, lightweight string or transparent tape, vase

Find 4 similar-size branches with several twigs coming off of them. Decorate each branch with the coloring of winter, spring, summer, and fall. Cut snowflakes, flowers, bugs, and leaves from construction paper. Decorate them with markers or colored pencils. Tie or tape the shapes on each branch for each of the 4 seasons. Arrange the branches in a pretty vase to make a colorful centerpiece for a table.

BAND: KAZOO

268

You don't need years of practice to make beautiful music. All you need is this kazoo and a good song to hum.

What You'll Need: Paper towel tube, markers, waxed paper, scissors, rubber band

Decorate the paper towel tube with markers. Make it match the rest of your band instruments with palm trees or wild stripes and colors. Wrap a piece of waxed paper over one end of the tube. Secure it with a rubber band. Have an adult cut 2 holes in the tube. To play your kazoo, hum your favorite song into the open end of the tube. Make more kazoos with tubes that have different diameters, thicknesses, and lengths to create various sounds.

KEEPSAKE ORNAMENTS

269

Create an original ornament every holiday season to record your years as a budding artist.

What You'll Need: Round wood plaque (available at craft stores), permanent markers or acrylic paints and paintbrush, ribbon

Draw or paint a holiday design on a wood plaque. Here are some ideas for designs based on geometric shapes: a triangle tree, a circle wreath, a square present, and a diamond holly leaf. Use a combination of shapes to make a picture of Santa Claus. If you use paint, let it dry. Sign your work and write the date. Thread a piece of ribbon through the hole at the top of the wood plaque. Tie the ends in a knot to hang your ornament. Make a new one for each Christmas so that you'll have a record of your holiday artwork.

COUNTDOWN CALENDAR

270

Waiting for a special occasion can take forever, but this countdown calendar helps the time go faster.

What You'll Need: Construction paper, markers or colored pencils, blunt scissors, craft glue, removable tape

Make a window calendar to count the days until a special holiday or your birthday, or to celebrate each day of a longer holiday such as Hanukkah or Kwanza. For Hanukkah, draw a menorah with candles to count the 8 days of the holiday. Draw a flame above the center candle on the menorah. To make the countdown windows, cut 8 small rectangles from construction paper. Fold each one in half, and glue one above each candle. On the inside of the window, draw a candle flame. Close the window and secure it with a piece of removable tape. Write the number for the countdown day on the front of the window, working right to left for the 8 days of Hanukkah. Then open a window on each day of the celebration.

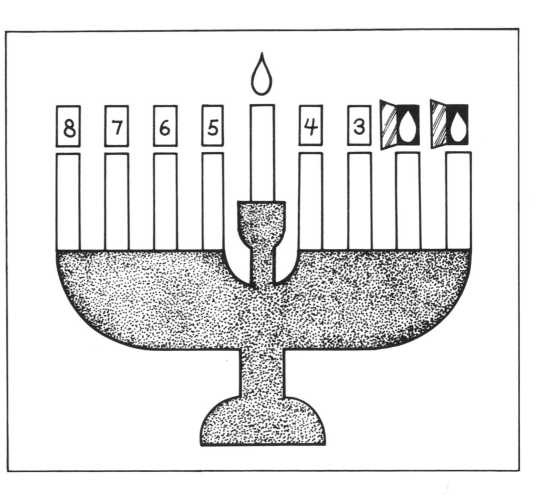

RAY STENCILS

271

Decorate a greeting card or make a holiday decoration with a simple scribble.

What You'll Need: Drawing paper, pencil, blunt scissors, coloring tools such as crayons or colored pencils

Fold a piece of drawing paper in half. Draw half of a heart shape on the fold. Cut out the heart shape along the lines. Here are a few designs you can make with the cutout heart shape and the cutout paper stencil. With the heart shape: Hold the cutout carefully on a piece of paper, and draw rays outward across the edge. With the stencil: Fill in the shape with horizontal or vertical lines, or draw small rays inward from the edge. You can make borders around a picture or overlap the hearts to make patterns. Cut out more shapes for other holidays. Use the shapes and stencils to make special greeting cards.

PUNCH-OUT ANGELS

272

When you place your angel carefully over a Christmas tree light, the magical effect will knock you out.

What You'll Need: Pencil, gold or silver craft foil, blunt scissors, foam sheet, pushpin, thread

Draw an angel pattern on a piece of gold or silver craft foil. Cut the angel shape out. Place the foil angel over a foam sheet. Use a pushpin to punch out lines of swirls in the angel's skirt, feather lines in her wings, a border on her gown, and hair on her head. Punch a hole in the foil for the hanger. String a piece of thread through the hole and knot the ends to make the hanger loop. Hang the foil angel on your tree near a light for a pretty, shimmery decoration.

Since craft foil comes in many different colors, you can combine the colors in a picture or make punch-out decorations for other holidays as well. Or instead of foil, punch decorations in greeting cards and paper sculptures, too.

VALENTINE IDEAS

273

Valentine's Day is a time to say you care about others. Show them how much with these heartfelt ideas.

What You'll Need: Doilies, blunt scissors, red and white construction paper, craft glue, glitter, satin ribbon, craft stick, plastic sandwich bag, valentine candy

Doily Cards: Cut heart shapes from doilies, and glue them on red and white construction paper hearts. Use glue to write *Be Mine* on the doily. Cover the glue with glitter. Tie satin ribbon in small bows, and glue them to the doily cards. Once the glue has dried, shake off the excess glitter.

Heart & Arrow Cards: Cut a heart shape from red construction paper. Cut a smaller heart from white construction paper and glue it on top of the red heart. Make an arrow from a craft stick and construction paper. Write a valentine for someone special. If you want, attach a plastic sandwich bag filled with valentine candy.

CRAFT FOAM ORNAMENTS

When you send a handmade ornament to someone special, it says, "I'm thinking of you."

274

What You'll Need: Assorted colors of craft foam sheets, ballpoint pen, blunt scissors, needle, poster paints, paper towels, thread

Draw a Christmas tree shape on a sheet of green craft foam, draw a Santa Claus shape on red craft foam, and draw a candle and candleholder on yellow craft foam. Cut out all the shapes. Use a needle to scratch in the detail on both sides of each foam shape. Rub poster paint in the scratched areas. Wipe off any excess paint with a damp paper towel. Carefully poke a small hole in the top of each foam shape. String a piece of thread through each hole and knot the ends to make the hanger loop.

I HAVE A DREAM

275

Dr. Martin Luther King, Jr., had a dream for his country. What are your dreams for the future?

What You'll Need: Drawing paper, markers or colored pencils, two 9-inch wood dowels, transparent tape

On January 18, the United States celebrates the vision of Dr. Martin Luther King, Jr. Personalize his message by making your own list of dreams. Use markers or colored pencils to write your dreams on a piece of drawing paper. Some of your dreams may be serious and some may be silly. Draw a picture to illustrate each dream you write down. If one of your dreams is for clean air, water, and earth, then draw the world. After you have written down your dreams, display them on a scroll. Tape a wood dowel to each edge of the paper.

WIRE SANTA

276

Twist, wrap, and shape your way into the holiday spirit by creating your very own version of Santa.

What You'll Need: Plastic coated wire or green floral wire (both available at craft stores), stapler and staples, cardboard

Start by twisting the wire to make a face and a beard. Remember this sculpture is a bit abstract so you don't need to add a lot of detail. Next move down to make the neck, arms, and body. First make the line of the body part, such as the arm, then make loopy twists of wire around it. Continue with the rest of the figure, twisting the wire around to make the legs and boots. Keep looping the wire back and forth, around and around, until the figure has the shape you like. When you're finished, bend the arms and legs to make an interesting position. To display the wire Santa, staple the figure to a piece of cardboard.

POP-UP HOLIDAY CARD

277

Nothing says "You're special" better than a card with wishes from the heart, especially one with a pop-up surprise.

What You'll Need: Construction paper, ruler, pencil, blunt scissors, craft glue, markers

1. Fold a piece of construction paper in half, making a strong crease. Draw half of a heart shape at the fold. Halfway down the heart shape, make 2 pencil marks about 1 inch apart.

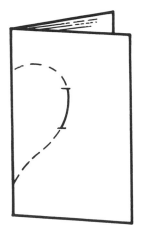

2. Cut from the top of the heart to the top mark. Then cut from the bottom of the heart to the bottom mark.

3. Fold the cut flap back and forth several times to crease it well. Bring the flap back to center. Unfold the page almost completely, and gently push the flap through to the other side. You should have a heart that pops out of the paper.

4. To make a pop-up valentine card, fold another piece of construction paper in half. Trim the pop-up piece of paper so that it is slightly smaller than the folded construction paper. Glue the back of the pop-up paper to the inside of the larger paper. Decorate the front of your greeting card, and write a valentine message inside.

BALANCING ACT MOBILE

278

Notice that one heavy and one light object can still balance, depending on where you position the items.

What You'll Need: 1½ yards of yarn; blunt scissors; one 12-inch wood dowel with ¼-inch diameter; two 6-inch wood dowels with ¼-inch diameter; natural items such as shells, bark, and rocks

Cut the following pieces of yarn: one 15-inch, one 9-inch, five 5-inch, and one 4-inch. Tie one end of the 15-inch piece of yarn to the center of the 12-inch dowel to hang the mobile. Tie one end of the 9-inch yarn piece to the center of one 6-inch dowel. Tie the other end of the yarn piece to one end of the 12-inch dowel. Tie one end of a 5-inch yarn piece to the center of the remaining 6-inch dowel. Tie the other end of the yarn to the other end of the 12-inch dowel. Tie the 4-inch yarn piece to the center of the 12-inch dowel. Tie the remaining 5-inch yarn pieces to the 6-inch dowels. Hang natural items such as shells, bark, and rocks on the yarn ends to balance the mobile.

STRAW GLIDER

279

With a little help from the wind, your straw glider will take to the air and soar across the sky.

What You'll Need: 3 plastic drinking straws, masking tape, pencil, craft foam or clean foam food trays (from fruits or vegetables only), blunt scissors, permanent markers, glue

Tape 3 straws together at 4 points. Draw the wing and 2 tail sections on a piece of craft foam or foam food trays. Cut out the pieces and decorate them with markers. Draw a design of your own airline company. Insert the foam pieces in between the 3 straws. Add a dab of glue to hold them in place. Let the glue set. Hold the glider in one hand, then throw it in the air and watch it fly.

PAPER CHAINS

280

Link the colors of your favorite holiday to create a festive decoration or countdown chain.

What You'll Need: Assorted colors of construction paper, blunt scissors, ruler, transparent tape or craft glue, ornament with paper clip hook (optional)

Cut several 1×5-inch strips of construction paper using the colors of the holiday you are celebrating. The number of strips depends on how long you want the chain to be. With one strip, bring the ends together to form a circle. Tape or glue the ends in place. Insert another strip through the paper circle. Bring the ends together, forming a linked circle. Tape or glue the ends in place. Repeat this procedure to continue the chain, making sure you link the strips.

Use a red and green chain to decorate a Christmas tree or a pink and yellow chain to decorate your door at Easter. You can also use the chains to count down the days until a special holiday. Make a red and green paper chain to count down Christmas. Be sure to number each link for each day. Move an ornament with a paper clip hook along the numbered chain each day until you get to the last link.

SPRING BUNNY

281

Make a funny bunny with paper springs, and watch it wiggle, wave, and hop to life.

What You'll Need: Construction paper, ruler, blunt scissors, transparent tape, markers, craft glue, cotton ball or white pom-pom

Cut two 1×8-inch strips of construction paper. Tape one end of each strip together into an L-shape. Fold the bottom strip back over the top strip. Fold the other strip back over the last strip. Continue folding the strips back and forth to make a spring. When you get to the end of the strips, tape the ends together to hold them in place. Make 3 more springs.

Draw a bunny shape on a piece of construction paper. Draw in the bunny's features. Glue each spring to the bunny's body for arms and legs. Draw 2 paws and 2 feet on a piece of construction paper and cut them out. Glue the paws and feet to the spring ends. Glue a cotton ball or pom-pom to the back of the bunny for the tail. Place your spring bunny in an Easter basket, or hang it on the wall.

EGG HOLDERS

282

Display your Easter eggs proudly with these animated egg holders. They make a nice surprise for the Easter bunny.

What You'll Need: Construction paper, markers or colored pencils, ruler, blunt scissors, transparent tape

Draw a baby chick with extended strips for "wings" and "feet" on a piece of construction paper. The strips should be at least 7 inches long. Color in the baby chick's features using markers or colored pencils. Cut the chick shape out. If you want, trim the wing strip so that the edge is scalloped to make "feathers." Tape the ends of the feet strip together. Stand an Easter egg in the ring. Tape the ends of the wing strip together to "hug" the egg. Make other animal shapes to hold more eggs.

EASTER EGGS

283

Here's a recipe for a different kind of Easter egg. You can create a natural dye using onion skins.

What You'll Need: Cheesecloth, ruler, blunt scissors, one dozen eggs, leafy herbs such as parsley or coriander, assorted onion skins (red, brown, white, yellow), cotton string

Cut the cheesecloth into 6-inch squares. Take an egg in your hand and place an herb on the egg. Holding the herb in place, wrap a large onion skin around the egg. Place more herbs around the egg and wrap another onion skin around it. Place the covered egg on a square of cheesecloth. Tightly wrap the cheesecloth around the egg. Tie it closed with a piece of cotton string. Repeat the process to make more eggs. Have an adult help you boil the eggs in water for 20 to 30 minutes. Take the eggs out of the water and allow them to cool. Unwrap the eggs and display them in baskets or egg holders.

FANCY FLOWERPOT

284

Design your own painted flowerpot to show off a beautiful plant or floral arrangement.

What You'll Need: Clay flowerpot, dish detergent, newspaper, pencil, acrylic paints, paintbrush

Wash the flowerpot, even if it is new, with dish detergent. Rinse it thoroughly, and place it in the sun to dry. Cover your work surface with newspaper. Sketch a pattern or picture on the flowerpot. You can draw an apple pattern, a picture of your family, or an abstract design. Paint it with acrylic paints. Let the paint dry. Once the paint is dry, put a plant in the flowerpot.

DOILY BASKETS

285

You can use these delicate baskets to hold Easter candy or a special Easter gift.

What You'll Need: Square or rectangular doilies, transparent tape, construction paper, blunt scissors, craft glue, green plastic grass

Fold in the 4 sides of a doily. Stand the sides up, pinching the corners in as you unfold the sides. Hold the pinched corners in place with tape. Cut a strip of construction paper to make a handle for the doily basket. Cut and glue pieces of doily lace to the handle. Tape the ends of the handle to the inside of the basket. Fill your basket with some green "grass" and holiday goodies. These lacy baskets also make great party favors. Make one for each guest and fill it with treats.

FLY A KITE

286

Let your kite soar on a windy day. In between flights, use your bedroom wall as a hangar.

What You'll Need: One 12-inch wood dowel with ⅛-inch diameter, one 24-inch wood dowel with ⅛-inch diameter, strong string or cord, ruler, blunt scissors, wrapping paper, craft glue, colored tissue paper

1. Make a cross with the wood dowels. The longer dowel should be positioned vertically. Use a piece of strong string or cord to tightly tie the 2 dowels together at the cross section. Cut a piece of wrapping paper in a 16×28-inch diamond shape. Cut off the corners to make the tabs as shown. Place the crossed dowels in the center of the paper diamond.

2. Put a dot of glue at the end of each dowel. Run a long piece of string around the dowel frame through the glue. Add another dot of glue to each end to cover the string. Let the glue set. Fold the wrapping paper tabs over the string and glue each tab in place. Let the glue set.

3. To make the flight cord, cut a piece of string and tie each end to the horizontal dowel. To make the kite string, cut a long piece of string and tie it to the center of the flight cord. Tie a piece of string to the bottom of the vertical dowel for the kite tail. Make tissue paper bows to fold over the string and glue in place. Let the glue dry, then fly your kite!

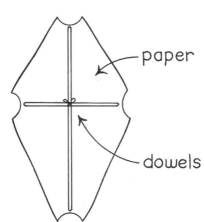

Place crossed dowels on top of paper.

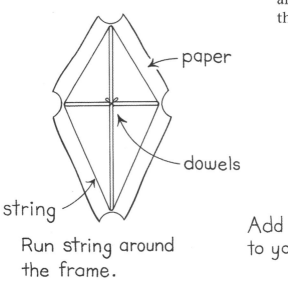

Run string around the frame.

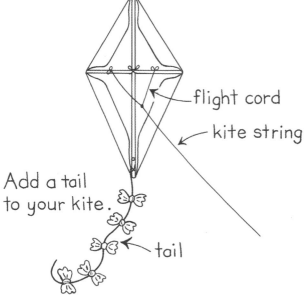

Add a tail to your kite.

PINWHEELS

287

When your pinwheel catches the wind, the colors come alive as they spin and swirl in the breeze.

What You'll Need: Two different colors of lightweight paper, blunt scissors, ruler, small nail, hammer, 12-inch wood dowel with ¼-inch diameter

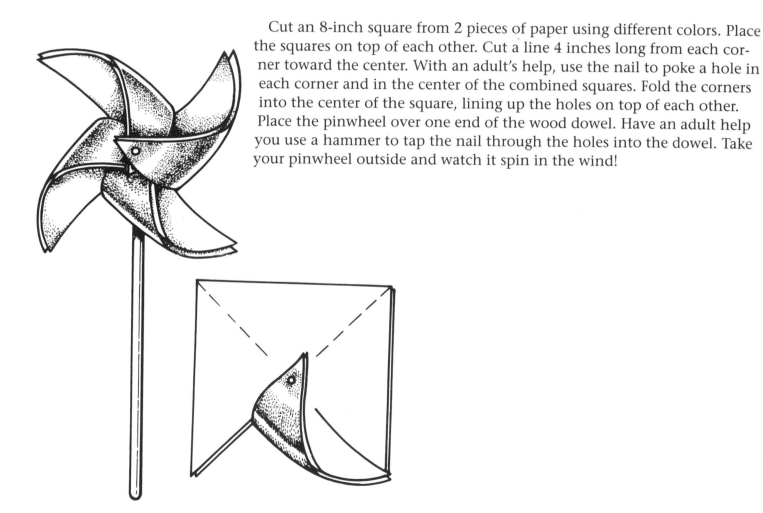

Cut an 8-inch square from 2 pieces of paper using different colors. Place the squares on top of each other. Cut a line 4 inches long from each corner toward the center. With an adult's help, use the nail to poke a hole in each corner and in the center of the combined squares. Fold the corners into the center of the square, lining up the holes on top of each other. Place the pinwheel over one end of the wood dowel. Have an adult help you use a hammer to tap the nail through the holes into the dowel. Take your pinwheel outside and watch it spin in the wind!

SAILBOATS

288

Sailboat racing is a time-honored sport. Make your own swimming pool competition with these tiny floating boats.

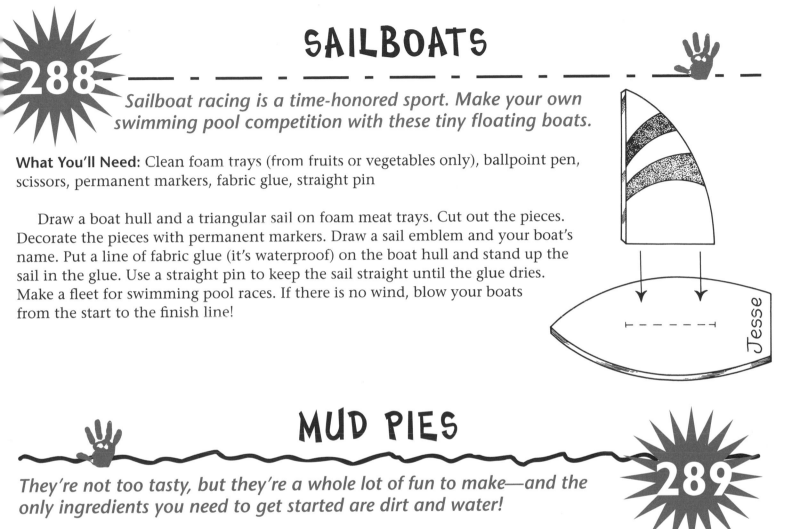

What You'll Need: Clean foam trays (from fruits or vegetables only), ballpoint pen, scissors, permanent markers, fabric glue, straight pin

Draw a boat hull and a triangular sail on foam meat trays. Cut out the pieces. Decorate the pieces with permanent markers. Draw a sail emblem and your boat's name. Put a line of fabric glue (it's waterproof) on the boat hull and stand up the sail in the glue. Use a straight pin to keep the sail straight until the glue dries. Make a fleet for swimming pool races. If there is no wind, blow your boats from the start to the finish line!

MUD PIES

289

They're not too tasty, but they're a whole lot of fun to make—and the only ingredients you need to get started are dirt and water!

What You'll Need: Old clothes; throwaway containers; plastic spoon; dirt and water; grass; disposable pie pans; leaves; natural items from the yard such as seeds, flowers, and twigs

Put on some old clothes. Mix some dirt and water in a throwaway container to make mud. Mix in some grass to add texture to the mud. Line a disposable pie pan with leaves. Pour some mud into the pan over the leaves. Sprinkle your mud pie with seeds, and add flowers or twigs to decorate it. Let the mud set until it dries. Make more pies with your friends and pretend you have an outdoor bakery. "Sell" the mud pies to your friends and family members.

RAINBOW FLOWERPOT

290

*You don't need to wait for a rainstorm in order to find a rainbow.
This rainbow pot adds color to any plant.*

What You'll Need: 6-inch clay flowerpot; dish detergent; craft glue; old paintbrush; yarn in the following colors: red, orange, yellow, green, blue, and violet

Wash the flowerpot, even if it is new, with dish detergent. Rinse it thoroughly, and place it in the sun to dry. Apply a 1-inch band of glue around the base of the flowerpot. Wrap violet yarn around the flowerpot, covering the band of glue. Apply another band of glue around the flowerpot above the violet yarn. Wrap the next rainbow color, blue, around the pot. Continue gluing and wrapping the yarn up the flowerpot until it's covered completely. Let the glue set, then put a plant in the flowerpot.

SPECIAL TABLECLOTHS

291

Add some color to the dinner table with special tablecloths you make yourself.

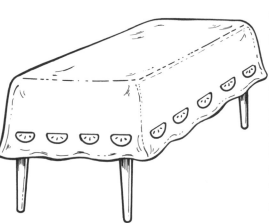

What You'll Need: Paper tablecloth, markers, blunt scissors or pinking shears

Make a special tablecloth for your dinner table. Color a paper tablecloth with markers. Decorate it with your favorite foods such as pizza, ice cream cones, or fried chicken. For a Fourth of July picnic, find out what's on the menu. Draw a border of corn-on-the-cob, hamburgers and hot dogs, or watermelon slices. You can even cut a special design in the edges with scissors or pinking shears. If you want, place your tablecloth over a bright-colored tablecloth to show off the decorative edge.

PARACHUTE

292

When the spring winds blow, get out your parachutes and let Mother Nature help you play a game.

What You'll Need: Pencil, ruler, heavyweight paper, blunt scissors, thin cotton or nylon cloth, markers, cotton string, action figure

Here's an easy way to make a hexagon. Draw and cut out a triangle with 14-inch sides from a piece of heavyweight paper. Trace it on the cloth, then set the heavyweight paper triangle on top of the original tracing so that a hexagon is formed. Trace it and cut it out. Use markers to write the name of your skydiving company with an insignia on the parachute. Cut a tiny hole in each corner. Tie 2 ends of each string in a knot through each hole. Hold all the strings together and make a slipknot 7 inches from the cloth parachute. Tie an action figure on the ends of the string. Bunch up the fabric and throw it up in the air. Watch the parachute float back to you.

BIKE SPECTACLE

293

Get together with the kids on your block and decorate your bikes for a neighborhood parade.

What You'll Need: Newspaper, blunt scissors, ruler, masking tape, colored tissue paper, twist tie

Decorate your bike with pom-poms, paper fringe, and flowers. To make pom-poms, fanfold 2 pages of newspaper together. Make a long cut through each crease to about 3 inches from the end. Wrap tape around the uncut end. Repeat to make another pom-pom. Tape the pom-pom to your handlebars. To make paper fringe, cut a 9-inch-wide strip of colored tissue paper. Fold it in half lengthwise. Cut slits along the open edge about ½ inch apart up to about 2 inches from the folded edge. Tape the fringe around the bars on your bike. To make flowers, cut 3 large circles from colored tissue paper. Place the circles on top of each other and gather them in the middle so that they look like a bow. Secure the centers with a twist tie. Separate the paper layers and fluff it into a flower. Tape the flower to the front of your handlebars.

FIREWORKS PICTURE

294

After you experience the spectacular display of the Fourth of July fireworks, re-create the colorful bursts and blasts in a picture.

What You'll Need: Assorted colors of construction paper, blunt scissors, craft glue, black construction paper, hole punch, aluminum foil

Cut building shapes from assorted colors of construction paper. Cut out skyscrapers, small buildings, or houses to match your town. To make your town's skyline, glue the building shapes along the bottom of the black construction paper sheet. Use a hole punch to make confetti dots from aluminum foil and assorted colors of construction paper. Glue the colored dots over the nighttime skyline to re-create a magnificent fireworks display.

SIDEWALK ART

295

Create a sidewalk gallery for your neighbors. They'll be able to enjoy your artwork while they walk.

What You'll Need: Colored chalk, safe sidewalk or concrete driveway, paper towel

Find a safe sidewalk area away from traffic. (Be sure to ask permission to draw on the sidewalk.) Use colored chalk to draw your art on the sidewalk. Try chalking a sunset. Start at the top with blues, then add purples, reds, and oranges. Work in some fluffy pink-tinted clouds. Finish up with some snowcapped mountains. Rub a paper towel across the edges of your colors to blend them. Instead of a square picture, be creative with your concrete space. Chalk a long skinny dragon down the sidewalk or a school of fish on a concrete walkway. Another idea is to trace the shadow of an object, such as a tree, on the concrete. Then, color in the outline.

PAPER AIRPLANE FOLDING

296

Fold and decorate an entire fleet of airplanes that spiral and glide through the air.

What You'll Need: Construction paper, markers

1. Fold a sheet of construction paper in half lengthwise. Open it back up and fold the bottom corners up to the center crease.

2. Fold each diagonal end in to the center crease.

3. Refold the paper in half again at the center crease.

4. Fold the top right end back to the folded edge. Flip the paper airplane over, and fold the top left end back to the folded edge. Decorate your jet with an insignia, a camouflage pattern, or a wild and crazy design.

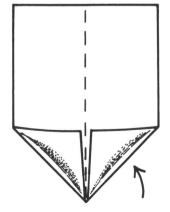 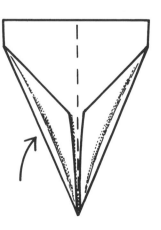 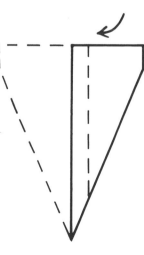 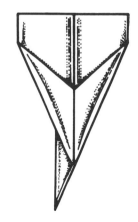

CLOTHESLINE BASKETRY

297

Colors swirl and coil around to create a soft basket that is perfect for holding all your secret treasures.

What You'll Need: Newspaper, food coloring, bowls (for the dye), 6 yards of clothesline, yarn, large bowl, blunt scissors, needlepoint needle

1. The first thing you need to do is dye the clothesline. It's best to do this outside. Cover your work surface with newspaper. To dye the clothesline, add food coloring to water using a different bowl for each color. Dip the clothesline in the bowls. Let the clothesline dry in the sun.

2. Begin by coiling the clothesline at one end. Tie 4 long pieces of yarn to the first coil.

3. As you continue wrapping the clothesline around the coil, overlap the yarn. Weave the yarn pieces over and under the coils to secure them in place. As you coil the clothesline up, place it in a large bowl to give your basket some form. This will also make it easier to coil the clothesline. Once you've coiled about 6 circles, add 4 more yarn ties to the clothesline. Continue to circle the coil and weave the yarn over and under the clothesline.

4. When you get to the end of the clothesline, trim any excess to make the last row of coil even with the rest. Tie the ends of the yarn pieces in a knot and trim the excess yarn. Thread a long piece of yarn through a needlepoint needle. Stitch the yarn around the last 2 coils of clothesline.

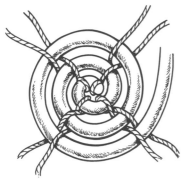

Coil one end of clothesline, and tie four pieces of yarn to coil.

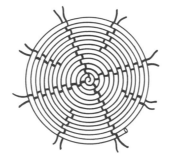

As you coil clothsline, weave yarn over and under it to secure.

Stitch yarn around the last two coils of clothesline.

SUNDIAL

298

As the sun moves throughout the day, so does the shadow it casts. A sun clock tells the time by the position of the shadow.

What You'll Need: Newspaper, colored poster board, blunt scissors, large plastic coffee can lid, plaster of paris, markers

Cover your work surface with newspaper. Cut a triangle from colored poster board. Have an adult help you mix the plaster of paris according to package directions. Carefully pour the plaster into the plastic coffee can lid. Stand the triangle up in the plaster. Let the plaster dry.

Use your sundial to tell the time. Take the sundial outside early on a sunny day. Place it where the sun will hit it all day. Every hour on the hour, make a mark at the shadow of the triangle. Write the hour on the plaster. Once you've marked off the hours, keep your sundial in the same spot so you can tell the time on sunny days.

TOE PAINTING

299

Create a work of art with your feet. Play some tunes, dip your feet in paint, and tap your toes to the music's beat.

What You'll Need: Newspaper, large piece of drawing paper, masking tape, finger paints, paper plate, bucket, old towel

Cover your work surface with newspaper. Place a chair on top of the newspaper. Pour the finger paints on paper plates. Arrange them within close reach of the chair. Fill a bucket with warm water and place it next to the chair. Tape a large piece of paper to the newspaper in front of the chair, then sit in the chair. Dip your big toe in the paint and make a design on the paper. Paint heel prints and dots with your toes. Dip your feet in the water to rinse the paint off your foot. Dry your foot with an old, clean towel.

CORNUCOPIA COPIES

300

A cornucopia is a horn of plenty. Make yours overflow with fruit and flowers, plus plenty of color and texture.

What You'll Need: Pencil, corrugated cardboard, blunt scissors, poster board, craft glue, newspaper, poster paints, palette or paint tray, brayer, drawing paper

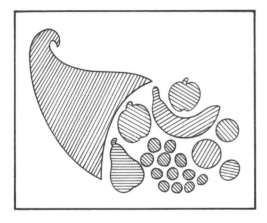

Draw a horn shape on a piece of corrugated cardboard. Draw fruit shapes such as a pear, a banana, grapes, and apples on cardboard. Carefully peel a layer of paper off the side of the cardboard you have not drawn on to expose the inside ridges. Cut out the shapes. Glue the horn on a piece of poster board. Glue the fruit shapes on the poster board in front of the horn. Let the glue set.

Cover your work surface with newspaper. Place poster paint on a palette or paint tray. Roll the brayer in the paint, then roll it over the cardboard shapes. Place a piece of paper over the painted surface. Gently rub the paper with your hands. Remove the paper and let the paint dry.

SQUIRT BOTTLE ART

301

Since the summer heat quickly dries your artwork, race your friends to see who can finish their picture the fastest.

What You'll Need: Clean plastic dish detergent bottles with a squirt lid, safe sidewalk or concrete driveway

Here's a project that's a lot of fun on a sunny day. Fill a plastic dish detergent bottle with water. Squirt the water to "draw" a picture on the sidewalk or driveway. Shade and color in your picture with the bottle's water. You must work very quickly before the sun "erases" your design. That's the fun part of this project. You get to start all over again.

302 PATRIOTIC COLLAGE

What does Independence Day mean to you? Gather up symbolic objects and create your own patriotic collage.

What You'll Need: Old magazines, blunt scissors, red, white, and blue fabric scraps, craft glue, construction paper

Look through old magazines for pictures of patriotic symbols such as the American flag, stars, bells, eagles, and historical monuments. You can also look for pictures of people saluting, soldiers marching, or lawmakers speaking. Cut out the pictures. Cut scraps of red, white, and blue fabric into stars and stripes. Glue the pictures and the fabric to a piece of construction paper in a random arrangement. Cover the sheet of paper with the pictures and fabric pieces overlapping. Let the glue dry.

CORNHUSK DOLL 303

Make a traditional cornhusk doll with Indian corn to celebrate the arrival of fall.

What You'll Need: One ear of Indian corn, yarn, craft stick or frozen treat stick, craft glue, black felt-tip pen

Bend the cornhusks on the ear of the Indian corn over the cob. Tie a piece of yarn around the husks about 2 inches from the top for the head. Tie another piece around the husks at the middle of the cob for the body. Insert a craft stick or frozen treat stick through the husks for the arms. Add a dab of glue to hold the arms in place. Draw a face on the husks. Glue yarn hair on top of the doll's head.

BOX COSTUME

304

Turn an oversized box into a great Halloween costume. Make animals, cars, buildings, or even furniture!

What You'll Need: Large cardboard box, scissors, markers, newspaper, poster paints, masking tape, wide cloth ribbon, stapler and staples

With an adult's help, cut the bottom and top off of a cardboard box. Use the top and bottom pieces to make a horse's head and tail for a carousel horse costume. Draw the shape of a horse's head and tail on the cardboard pieces. Decorate the shapes with markers and have an adult cut them out. Cover your work surface with newspaper. Paint the horse body with poster paints. After the paint has dried, tape the head and tail to the box body.

Make suspenders to hold the horse costume around your body. With an adult's help, staple a long piece of wide ribbon to one inside corner of the box. Staple the other end of the ribbon to the opposite inside corner. Staple a second piece of ribbon to the inside of the remaining corners so that the ribbon suspenders cross over one another.

SPIDERWEB PICTURES

305

Spiders can be scary, but don't be afraid of these creepy friends. Wherever you put them, that's where they'll stay.

What You'll Need: Construction paper, markers or colored pencils, craft glue, black pom-pom, 2 sequins

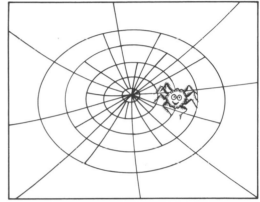

Draw a small circle in the middle of a sheet of construction paper. Draw another circle around it. Keep adding bigger circles until you have drawn 4 or 5 circles total. Draw lines from the center circle to the edges of the paper. Draw some lines from the center circle to the edges of the other inner circles. To make the spider, glue a black pom-pom to the web. Glue 2 sequins to the pom-pom for the eyes. Draw in the spider's 8 long legs. If you want, color in all the spaces in the web with bright colors to make it look like a stained glass web.

HALLOWEEN ORNAMENTS

306

Scare up a few of these recycled ornaments and start a new family tradition—Halloween trees!

What You'll Need: White plastic bags, ruler, blunt scissors, newspaper, black yarn, black permanent marker, orange fabric, old tennis ball

Here are some ideas for rainproof ornaments made with recyclables. To make a ghost, cut a 10- to 12-inch circle from a white plastic bag. Poke a tiny hole in the center. Crumple up a piece of newspaper into a tight ball. Tie black yarn around the ball. Pull the yarn through the hole on the plastic circle for the ornament hanger. Tie another piece of yarn around the plastic under the newspaper ball. Draw a ghost's face on the bag. To make a pumpkin, cut a circle from orange fabric. Wrap it around an old tennis ball. Tie it closed with yarn. Draw a face on the fabric. Hang your ornaments on a Halloween tree.

TRICK-OR-TREAT JUG

307

Design a rainproof candy jug to match your costume: a black cat jug for a witch or a treasure chest for a pirate.

What You'll Need: Plastic milk jug, scissors, permanent markers, black felt, craft glue, fabric markers, 2 screws, brass paper fasteners

With an adult's help, cut off the top half of a plastic milk jug. Set it aside. Decorate the bottom half of the milk jug to make a trick-or-treat basket. Use markers to draw on a Frankenstein face. Cut a strip of black felt for his hair. Glue it to the basket. Have an adult poke 2 holes near the bottom of the basket. Insert a screw in each hole for Frankenstein's bolts. Cut 2 small pieces of felt. Glue them over the ends of the screws on the inside of the basket. Cut a 1-inch-wide strip from the top half of the jug. Punch holes in the handle ends and the sides of the basket. Use brass paper fasteners to attach the handle to the basket.

HALLOWEEN MURAL

308

This mural is a fun way to tell picture stories. Ask friends to help out— there's space for everyone!

What You'll Need: Butcher paper or heavy wrapping paper, masking tape, newspaper, poster paints, paintbrushes

A mural is a large-size wall painting that tells a story or creates a scene. To make your holiday mural, tape a long piece of paper on the wall. Spread newspaper out along the floor. Starting at one end of the paper, paint a Halloween scene. Make a picket fence with jack-o'-lanterns, black cats, goblins, and a harvest moon. Add more items to "tell" a spooky or fun Halloween story. Follow your ideas right across the mural. Let the paint dry. This is a great project for a Halloween party. Have your friends each paint an area of the mural.

309 HALLOWEEN HOOD

This Halloween hood is not only a parent pleaser, but it's fun to wear!

What You'll Need: 12×18-inch piece of gray felt, black marker, blunt scissors, fabric glue, pink felt, 2 buttons, needle, gray thread, 6 pipe cleaners

1. Make a mouse costume with this hood. Fold the gray felt in half horizontally. Refer to the illustration to draw the hood, tie strings, and ear patterns on the felt. Follow the dimensions shown. Cut out all the pieces.

2. To make the hood, bring side A and side B of the hood piece together and glue them at the seam. Let the glue set. Cut a hole in each front corner of the hood. Thread the tie strings through the holes and tie the ends in a knot.

3. Glue the gray felt ears on the hood. Cut 2 inner ear pieces from pink felt and glue the pieces to the gray ears. Sew 2 buttons on the hood at the front rim for the eyes. Glue 3 pipe cleaners on each side for whiskers.

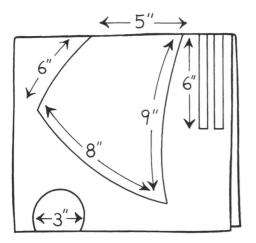

Cut out the felt pieces.

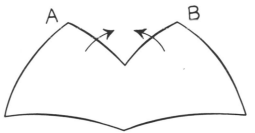

Bring side A and side B together.

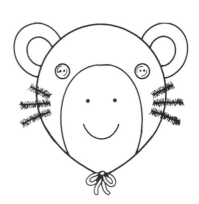

Decorate the hood with felt ears, button eyes, and whiskers.

WOVEN PUMPKIN

310

Make something different for Halloween this year. Weave a 3-dimensional pumpkin from construction paper.

What You'll Need: Orange and green construction paper, blunt scissors, transparent tape, pencil

1. Cut four 1×24-inch strips from orange construction paper. Arrange the strips as shown, overlapping them in the center. Secure the strips with tape.

2. To make a pumpkin sphere start with the bottom strip and bring the ends together to form a circle. Hold the ends in place with tape. Repeat with the remaining strips. Work from the bottom strip up and attach the ends together at the top of the sphere.

3. Draw a pumpkin stem shape on a piece of green construction paper. Cut out the stem, and tape it to the top of the pumpkin.

Arrange strips, overlapping the centers.

Tape ends of bottom strip together to form a circle.

Add a green paper stem to top of pumpkin sphere.

MASK ME

Whether your mask is silly or scary, no one will have a Halloween costume quite like yours.

What You'll Need: Paper plates, blunt scissors, pencil, markers, trims such as ribbon, pipe cleaners, and yarn, hole punch, craft glue, old sunglasses

Cut a paper plate in half. Hold the plate half up to your face and mark the position of your eyes. Cut out 2 holes for your eyes. Decorate the mask to look like an animal, a monster, or a fancy party mask. You can even trim the plate half into the shape of a cat or dog. Draw the features on the mask, and glue on trims such as yarn for hair. Punch a hole on each side of the mask. Cut 2 pieces of ribbon to tie the mask on. Another idea is to glue the mask to a pair of old sunglasses without lenses.

INDIAN CORN PAINTING

Indian corn makes great fall decorations, but did you know that it makes a great painting tool, too?

What You'll Need: Newspaper, poster paints, paper plates, 1 or 2 ears of Indian corn, sharp knife (use with an adult's supervision), drawing paper

Make a fall painting with Indian corn as your paintbrush. Cover your work surface with newspaper. Pour poster paint on some paper plates. Have an adult use a sharp knife to cut the corn into 3-inch sections. Dip the cut end of 1 corncob in poster paint. Stamp it on a piece of drawing paper to create a flowerlike pattern. Roll a 3-inch corncob in some poster paint. Then roll it on the paper for a unique dotted design. Use this technique to fill in a picture or to create patterned paper.

CANDLE SHIELD

313

Since you can't see the candle behind your shield, it will seem as if your picture is glowing all by itself.

What You'll Need: Heavy-duty aluminum foil, blunt scissors, ruler, permanent marker, pushpin, candle

1. Cut three 8-inch squares from the aluminum foil. Place the 3 foil squares on top of each other. Fold the edges over about 1 inch on each side.

2. Use a permanent marker to draw a design, such as a jack-o'-lantern, on the foil. Place the foil on a soft surface such as a rug or a piece of foam. Following the lines of the drawing, punch out the jack-o'-lantern design using a pushpin.

3. Curve the foil so that it stands up about 3 inches in the front of the candle. (Make sure there is a base under the candle to catch wax drips.) Have an adult light the candle.

Fold edges over.

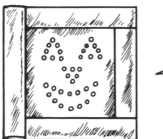

Punch out a design.

Place the shield in front of a candle.

FLYING DISK GAME

314

Don't let the rainy fall weather stop you from having fun. Play an exciting indoor game of Frisbee flying disk golf.

What You'll Need: 1-inch-thick urethane foam (available at fabric stores), blunt scissors, markers, transparent tape or string, 3 paper grocery bags, newspaper

To make the Frisbee flying disk, cut an 8-inch circle from the foam. Decorate it with markers. To make the golf targets, stuff 3 paper grocery bags with newspaper. Tape or tie the bags closed. Decorate the bags with funny faces or a bull's-eye design.

To play the game, place a target bag in a room and stand a distance away from it. Throw the foam disk until you hit the target. Count how many throws it takes to hit the target, and write down your score. Place the next bag in another room, and throw the disk. Finish the game with the third bag. Whoever has the lowest score wins.

SEASONAL SILHOUETTES

315

Think about each season's different colors and various holidays, then use these shades to make a collage.

What You'll Need: Colored tissue paper, craft glue, brown and black construction paper, white colored pencil, blunt scissors

Glue pieces of colored tissue paper—reds, oranges, and yellows for fall—all over a sheet of brown construction paper. Draw a fall shape on a piece of black construction paper using a white colored pencil. You might think of a tree, a pumpkin, cornucopia, or a ghost. Cut the shape out. Glue the silhouette over the tissue paper. Make a frame out of black construction paper, and glue it over the picture. Make other sheets with winter, spring, and summer colors and use black silhouettes to make a seasonal scene on the tissue paper. For a winter scene, cut out 2 children pulling a sled and some snowflakes falling.

HOBBY CRAFTS

Even if you aren't a carpenter, cook, tailor, or photographer, jump into the fun. The projects are simple and the results are impressive. You'll enjoy long hours of concentrated activity from projects such as the Motor Mat and the Flower Press. Be sure to have an adult help you with the cooking and carpentry projects. You can help mom or dad cut and drill all the wood pieces. The sewing projects can be made with a sewing machine, or they can be hand-stitched. The photography projects require a simple camera except for Ghost Pictures. The idea behind hobby crafts is to learn basic skills, learn to respect and handle tools, and have some fun.

CRISPY RICE ZOO

316

It won't take long for these delicious animals to become extinct. Not to worry, you can always make more.

What You'll Need: Crispy rice cereal, marshmallows, butter or margarine, waxed paper or aluminum foil, plastic sandwich bag

Have an adult help you make marshmallow treats following the recipe on the box of crispy rice cereal. Cover your work surface with a sheet of waxed paper or aluminum foil. Coat your hands in butter, or put a plastic sandwich bag coated with butter over your hands. While the mixture is still warm (be careful!), mold it into teddy bears, fish, ducks, and other round animals. Let the treats cool on waxed paper or foil.

TOTE IT

This tote is the most usable piece of art you'll ever create. You can even personalize it for yourself or a friend.

What You'll Need: 1 yard of bright-colored denim fabric, tape measure, scissors, sewing machine, iron-on fabric adhesive, iron and ironing board, fabric scraps, fabric paint

1. Have an adult help you with this project. Cut a 14×9-inch piece of denim fabric for the bag and a 3×15-inch piece for the handle. (To make a book bag, cut a 22×12-inch piece for the bag and a 24×3-inch piece for an over-the-shoulder handle.) Hem one 14-inch side on the larger piece of fabric. Fold the fabric in half with the seam of the hemmed edge facing out. Sew the two sides of the fabric together, running a stitch along the bottom and up the side of the folded fabric. Turn the bag inside out.

2. To make the tote bag handle, fold the 3×15-inch piece of fabric in thirds. Sew along the length of the fabric to stitch it together. Sew each end of the handle to the inside of the bag. Sew several stitches to secure the handle.

3. Decorate your bag with fabric. Iron the fabric adhesive to the back of some fabric scraps. Cut out shapes or a design from the fabric. Remove the paper backing from the adhesive. Place a fabric shape on the tote bag, and iron it in place. Continue decorating the tote bag with the remaining fabric shapes. Use fabric paint to outline the shapes or to add more shapes. Let the paint dry.

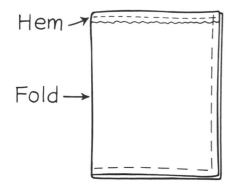

TERRIFIC TASSELS

318

Look around the house for objects that need a splash of color. Then decorate them with tassels.

What You'll Need: 2½-inch square of cardboard, yarn, blunt scissors

1. Wrap yarn around a 2½-inch square of cardboard 10 to 15 times. To make the tassel hanger, thread a piece of yarn under the wrapped yarn at the top edge of the cardboard. Bring the hanger ends together to form a loop and tie a knot to secure it. Carefully slip the wrapped yarn loops off the cardboard.

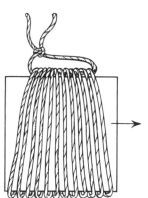

Slip the yarn loops off the cardboard.

2. Tie another piece of yarn around the top third of the yarn loops. Cut the loops at the bottom to make the tassel.

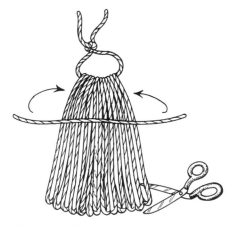

Cut the loops at the bottom.

3. Repeat steps 1 and 2 to make more tassels. Use the tassels to decorate shoes, barrettes, bicycle handlebars, place mats, hats, and more. Make two-color tassels in your school's team colors.

Use tassels to decorate shoes, barrettes, and more.

FANTASY PHOTOS

319

Tell a story with pictures. Create an adventure in which you play all the parts of the story.

What You'll Need: Camera, color film, blunt scissors, craft glue, poster board, markers

Plan a setting for your story. Think of a scene where there are lots of people doing different things, such as a circus or a football game. Have a family member or friend take several pictures of you dressed as the different parts of the story. For the circus, pose as a ringmaster, an acrobat, a clown, and even a lion. Dress up in costumes to fit the roles. When the film is developed, cut your pictures out and glue them on a piece of poster board. Draw a circus scene with 3 rings, a trapeze, balls to juggle, a lion, and more.

GEO BOARD

320

Here's a project that never ends. Use this board over and over again to make pictures and geometric designs.

What You'll Need: White paper, blunt scissors, ruler, pencil, 10-inch square of 1-inch-thick wood, thirty-six 1-inch brass nails, hammer, assorted rubber bands

Cut a 10-inch square from a piece of paper. Mark a matrix of dots about 1 inch apart on the paper. Place the paper over the wood board. Push a pencil through the paper at each dot to mark the position of the nails. With an adult's help, hammer the nails about halfway in the board at each dot. Connect rubber bands around the nails to make designs, geometric shapes, or letters on the board. Once you're done, remove the rubber bands so they won't get stretched out.

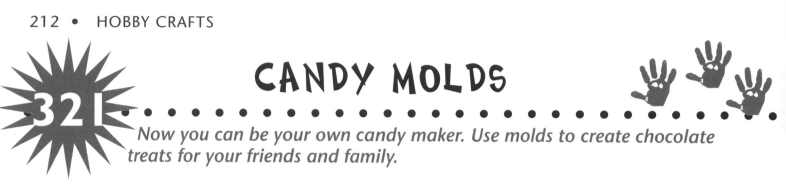

CANDY MOLDS

Now you can be your own candy maker. Use molds to create chocolate treats for your friends and family.

What You'll Need: Aluminum foil, ruler, blunt scissors, chocolate chips, measuring spoon

Cut several 4-inch squares from aluminum foil. Fold up the edges to make a "dish" to hold the melted chocolate. Press your finger inside the dish and fold the foil around it. Form the foil in holiday shapes such as Christmas trees, pumpkins, and hearts. For each foil mold, you will need 1 tablespoon of chocolate chips. Have an adult melt the chocolate in the microwave until it's smooth and creamy. Carefully pour the melted chocolate into the molds. Let the chocolate cool for 2 or 3 hours. (If you want to speed up the cooling process, put the candy molds in the refrigerator.) Once the chocolate has hardened, peel the foil off the candy shape.

NO-STITCH PILLOWS

No one's home to help you use the sewing machine? Now you can create fluffy pillows all by yourself!

What You'll Need: ⅔ yard of fabric, blunt scissors, cotton batting, fabric glue, 1 yard of grosgrain ribbon, permanent markers

Cut a 20×24-inch piece of fabric. Roll a 12-inch strip of cotton batting. Place the batting on the wrong side of the fabric. Roll the fabric around the batting. Glue the end seam in place to close the roll. Cut the grosgrain ribbon in half. Tie each piece in a bow around each end of the fabric roll. Fringe the edges of the fabric. Use permanent markers to draw on your favorite candy flavor label to make the pillow look like taffy.

BLOCK BUILDINGS

323

Create your own miniature city with buildings that look just like the ones in your town.

What You'll Need: 2×2-inch and 2×3-inch wood boards, saw, sandpaper, ruler, markers, cardboard, blunt scissors, wood glue, paper towel tubes

Have an adult saw all the wood pieces. Make sure you sand the wood smooth. To make a house or store, saw a 2-inch piece from a 2×2-inch board. Draw windows, doors, and shingles on the wood. Cut a roof piece from cardboard and glue it to the wood. To make a tall building, saw a 6-inch piece from a 2×2-inch board and an 8-inch piece from a 2×3-inch board. Stand them up and draw on the windows of a bank or the balconies of an apartment. To make a barn, cut a 5-inch piece from a 2×3-inch board. Decorate it with markers. Place the wood piece on its side and add a cardboard roof and a paper towel tube silo.

FUZZY PHOTOS

324

You can make special effects just like in the movies by putting something over the camera lens.

What You'll Need: Heavy-duty plastic wrap, camera, color or black-and-white film, petroleum jelly

Stretch a piece of strong plastic wrap over the lens of your camera. Try to make the plastic wrap as smooth as possible without any wrinkles. Lightly rub a very thin coating of petroleum jelly over the plastic wrap. This technique creates a special effect with your photos. Take some pictures of different objects and people. Once the photos are developed, you'll notice they have a soft, fuzzy look.

PLAY FURNITURE

325

Create your very own home. Put a television in the bathroom, a fridge in your bedroom—use your imagination!

What You'll Need: Colored or natural blocks of wood, wood glue, permanent markers, fabric scraps

Design a couch, chair, table, television, and clock with blocks of wood. To make a couch, glue 3 blocks of wood together, side by side. Then glue 3 blocks of wood upright behind the first 3 blocks. Add a block of wood to each end for the arms of the couch. To make a chair, glue 2 blocks together in an L-shape. Draw a fabric pattern on the couch and chair. Make a table with 2 blocks of wood glued together in a T-shape. For the clock and television, draw the clock face and the television screen and dials on the wood blocks. Use fabric scraps for a rug and a tablecloth.

PAPER POCKETS

326

If you want your holiday or birthday cards to be really special, tuck your messages inside a playful paper pocket.

What You'll Need: Pencil, poster board, blunt scissors, hole punch, ruler, yarn or ribbon, markers, valentine candy

Draw a heart shape on a piece of poster board. Cut it out and trace another heart on the poster board. Cut the second piece out. Punch holes around the sides and bottom of both cards, making sure the holes line up with each other. The holes should be about ½ inch apart. Thread yarn or ribbon through the holes to stitch the pieces together. Tie a bow at each end. Decorate the outside of the pocket with markers and fill it with valentine candy.

327 GRAHAM CRACKER CABIN

*Don't huff and puff to blow the house down—
just eat it!*

What You'll Need: White frosting, small bowls, food coloring, heavy-duty paper plate, graham crackers, waxed paper, assorted candies (to decorate the cabin)

Put a bit of frosting in the small bowls and mix in some food coloring. Spread a base of frosting on a plate. It can be green grass or white snow. Lay 6 graham crackers flat on a piece of waxed paper. Use frosting to "paint" windows and doors on the graham crackers. Stand the graham crackers up in the frosting base to make the cabin shape. "Glue" the sides together with frosting. To make the roof, gently position more crackers on top of the cabin. "Glue" them in place with frosting. Decorate the cabin with assorted candies.

BALL GOWN DRESS-UPS 328

*Turn mom's old skirt into a long dress just for you to
dress up in.*

What You'll Need: An old skirt, blunt scissors, 14 inches of elastic, needle and thread, trims such as sequins, old jewelry, and lace

Ask your mom for an old skirt. Hold it up to you at your chest. The skirt should fall to the floor from under your arms. Cut the elastic in half. Sew a piece of elastic at the skirt's waistband to make a shoulder strap. Repeat with the second piece of elastic. Sew on sequins, old jewelry, and lace at the skirt top, the waistband, and the straps to decorate your dress.

FABRIC TUBES

329

These tube projects are just the beginning. When your creative juices are flowing, see how many more ideas you can come up with.

What You'll Need: 1 yard of fabric, blunt scissors, needle and thread, cotton batting, felt, 2 buttons, markers, ribbon

1. To make a snake, cut a 5×30-inch piece of fabric. Fold the fabric in half lengthwise with the wrong side of the fabric facing out. Sew a seam along the long end, then turn it inside out. Sew one end of the tube closed.

2. Stuff the fabric tube with batting at the open end. Sew the open end closed.

3. Cut a piece of felt for the tongue. Sew it to the snake. Sew on 2 buttons for the eyes. Use markers to decorate the snake.

4. To create a wreath, make 3 tubes just like the snake but use 3 different colors of fabric. Braid the tubes together, then sew the ends together forming a circle. Use ribbon to tie a bow around the ends. Make a bed bolster using an 18×54-inch piece of fabric. Repeat steps 1 and 2 to make the tube.

← sewing line
← fold line

Sew a seam along the long end.

Stuff it with batting.

Decorate the snake with a felt tongue and button eyes.

330 — PHOTO STATUES

You don't need wood or stone to create a statue—all you need is a photograph.

What You'll Need: Large color photograph, blunt scissors, pencil, foam core board, craft knife, craft glue

Find an enlarged photograph of a friend, family member, or yourself. Carefully cut around the outside edges of the photo's subject. Place the cutout photo on the foam core board and trace around it. With an adult's help, use the craft knife to cut the shape from the foam core board. Leave a straight edge at the bottom. Glue the photo on the board. Trim the edges to even it out. Make a stand with 2 rectangles of foam core board. Cut a slit in the middle of each board half way through. Cut 2 slits in the bottom of the photo statue. Insert each rectangle in the slits.

FRUIT PIZZAS — 331

Cold pizza never tasted so good! This fruity pie is the perfect summertime treat.

What You'll Need: Pita bread, yogurt, food coloring (optional), assorted fruits such as bananas, apples, kiwi, and peaches

Start with the pita bread base as your pizza crust. Spread yogurt over the pita bread for the sauce. If you want, add a few drops of food coloring to the yogurt to make a colorful sauce. Have an adult help you cut up pieces of assorted fruits to make the pizza toppings. Use bananas, apples, and kiwi instead of the pepperoni, mushrooms, or sausage.

Make a vegetable pizza, too. Use ranch dressing instead of yogurt for the sauce. Then substitute broccoli, carrots, and tomatoes for the toppings.

PASTRY BAG

332

A pastry bag makes a great frosting tool to easily decorate cookies, cakes, and more.

What You'll Need: White frosting, small plastic sandwich bags, food coloring, blunt scissors

Divide the white frosting into small plastic sandwich bags. Add some food coloring to each bag. Knead the frosting in the bag to mix the color. Squeeze all the frosting toward a bottom corner. Cut a tiny piece off the corner of the bag. To decorate cakes or cookies, squeeze the frosting out of the hole. Use the pastry bag to make lines, draw faces, create holiday designs, or write names.

MOTOR MAT

333

With your motor mat, you can drive yourself to the movies, mall, or any other place you want to go.

What You'll Need: 1¼ yard of vinyl fabric, blunt scissors, tape measure, cord, permanent markers

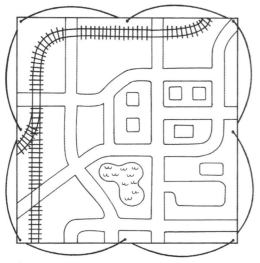

Cut a 40-inch square of vinyl fabric. Cut holes in the fabric and string cord in and out of each hole as shown in the illustration. Use permanent markers to draw roads, rivers, and railroads on one side of the vinyl fabric. Start in the middle and work out. Let the markers dry before you play. Make roads just like the ones in your neighborhood. Add parking places, a pond, and squares where wooden buildings might be placed. Use a green marker to draw trees and bushes. Let the markers dry. Use the Traffic Signs on page 237, the Gas Pump on page 125, and the Block Buildings on page 213 with your mat. When you're done playing, pull the cord to close the mat into a bag.

SOFT DOLL

334

These little handmade dolls are extra special. After all, you made them yourself!

What You'll Need: Muslin, pencil, scissors, needle and thread, cotton batting, fabric paint, yarn, felt

Fold the muslin in half. Draw a cookie-cutter doll shape on the muslin. Have an adult cut out the shape; you should have 2 pieces. Sew them together leaving 3 inches open at the top of the head. Cut a slit to the seam at the armpits, neck, and between the legs. Turn the fabric inside out. Stuff it with cotton batting. Sew the head closed. Use fabric paint to draw on the face. Sew on yarn for the hair. Make an outfit for your doll from felt.

SOFT PRETZEL FISH

335

Bet you've never tasted fish like this before! These salty creatures are a savory treat.

What You'll Need: 1 tablespoon yeast, 1½ cups warm water, ¾ teaspoon salt, 1½ teaspoons sugar, 4 cups flour, cookie sheet, aluminum foil, 1 egg, pastry brush

To make the pretzels, mix the yeast with water. Mix in the salt and sugar. Then add the flour. Knead the dough. Use your hands to roll pieces of the dough into long ropes. Shape them into all kinds of fish. Place a sheet of aluminum foil on the cookie sheet and sprinkle it with flour. Put the pretzel fish on the foil. Beat 1 egg in a small bowl. Brush the beaten egg over the pretzels, then sprinkle some salt on them. With an adult's help, bake the pretzels in the oven at 400 degrees Fahrenheit for about 30 minutes.

WIND SOCK

336

Hang your wind sock on the porch, and watch it dance and swing as it catches the breeze.

What You'll Need: One 26-ounce-size plastic coffee can lid, blunt scissors, ⅔ yard of nylon material, tape measure, permanent markers, needle and thread, cord

Have an adult cut the center out from the plastic coffee can lid to make a rim. Cut a piece of nylon 15 inches wide on one end, 17 inches wide on the other end, and 12 inches long. Decorate the fabric with permanent markers. Sew the 12-inch long ends together to form a tube. Fold the 17-inch wide end over the plastic rim. Sew a stitch around the rim to secure it.

To add streamers, cut four 1½×24-inch strips of nylon. Sew them to the 15-inch-wide end of the wind sock. To hang the wind sock, cut a 12-inch piece and a 15-inch piece of cord. Carefully cut 2 small holes in the fabric on opposite sides at the 17-inch-wide end. Tie on the cords, then tie the ends together. Hang it from the porch so that it is slightly angled to catch the wind.

FRUIT ROLL-UP COLLAGE

337

This treat is fun to make, cool to look at, and delicious to eat. What more could you want from a snack?

What You'll Need: Waxed paper, fruit roll-ups, blunt scissors

Cover your work surface with waxed paper. Unroll the fruit sheets. With clean scissors, cut the sheets into fun shapes. Arrange the fruit shapes on the waxed paper to make a football player, a flower bouquet, or the letters of your name. Then eat the yummy collage!

GHOST PICTURES

338

With a little clever trickery, you can make the camera see things that aren't really there, such as a ghost.

What You'll Need: White sheet, flashlight, camera, black-and-white film, markers, construction paper

Have a friend or family member wear a white sheet. Shine a flashlight on the "ghost." Set the camera on the table. Look through the lens and adjust the position of the camera so that the ghost is toward the left in the viewfinder. Set the shutter speed for one second. Now turn off all the lights in the room. Push the camera button to take a picture, then move the camera slightly. Take more ghost pictures. This time instead of moving the camera, tell the "ghost" to move very slowly. Draw a picture of a haunted house, then add the ghostly photos to your picture.

CLOTH PLACE MATS

339

Place mats add a festive touch to your holiday table. Make extras to put under the bread basket and fruit bowl.

What You'll Need: 2¼ yards of cotton fabric, tape measure, blunt scissors, felt, needle and thread

Cut four 12×16-inch pieces of fabric. Fray the ends or sew a hem to trim the edges. To fray the ends, pull out a few threads so it looks like fringe. To make a hem, sew the short ends over about 1 inch. Cut a piece of felt in a holiday design such as a turkey, Star of David, or Christmas tree. Sew the felt shape to the bottom right side of the place mat on three sides to make a pocket for the utensils. Insert a fork, knife, and spoon in the pocket when you set the table.

MEASURE ME STRIP

340

This strip takes only a short time to make, but it gives you years and years of measuring fun.

What You'll Need: 1×4-inch pine board about 6 feet long, permanent markers, yardstick, camera, color film, blunt scissors, craft glue

Draw a scale of inch and foot marks on one side of the pine board. Stand the board up in a corner of your room. Each time you measure yourself, write the date at the measurement mark. Add your baby measurements on the board, too. You can get the measurements from your pediatrician. Have a family member take a picture of you each time you measure yourself. Once the film is developed, cut the picture out and glue the photo to the board next to your measurement mark.

BED BANNER

341

Every night before bed, admire your banner to ensure good dreams throughout the night.

What You'll Need: 36×48-inch piece of felt, fabric glue, two 36-inch wood dowels with ½-inch diameter, 4 large wood beads, fabric and felt scraps, blunt scissors, yarn or string

Fold both shorter ends of the felt over about 2 inches, and glue in place to form pockets. Insert a dowel through each pocket, then glue the beads on each end. Cut pieces of fabric and felt to make a picture. Do you dream of being an astronaut, a ballet dancer, or a basketball player? Cut out shapes to match your dreams. Apply a thin film of glue on the back of each cutout shape. Assemble the pieces on the felt banner to make your picture. Tie a piece of yarn or string to the ends of the top dowel. Hang the banner above your bed.

T-SHIRT PILLOWS

Turn your favorite T-shirt into a huggable pillow.
It's so easy, you'll want to make a set.

What You'll Need: T-shirt, needle and thread, cotton batting

Find a T-shirt with a fun picture on it. Ask for permission to stitch the bottom and the sleeves closed. Stuff your pillow through the neck opening with cotton batting. Then sew the neck closed. Make a set of pillows for your room. If you have a plain T-shirt, make it into a custom pillow with your own design. See the Tie-Dye T-Shirt on page 60 or Shirt Painting on page 27.

NEDLEPOINT

Needlepoint is a wonderful project to do on rainy or snowy afternoons.
It turns indoor time into fun time.

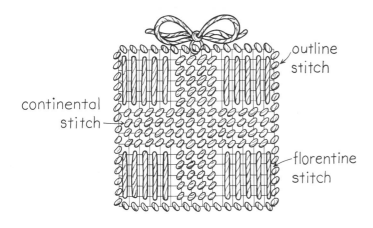

outline stitch

continental stitch

florentine stitch

What You'll Need: Plastic canvas (available at craft stores), scissors, yarn, needlepoint needle

Before you start, practice these 3 basic needlepoint stitches. The continental stitch is a diagonal stitch. The florentine stitch is a straight up and down or across stitch. It covers 1 or more squares. The outline stitch is an edging stitch around the plastic canvas.

To make a Christmas present ornament, have an adult trim the plastic canvas into a 4-inch square. Thread one end of the yarn through the needle, and tie the other end in a double knot. Start with the continental stitch for the present's ribbon. Fill in the present with the florentine stitch, then finish the edges with the outline stitch. When you've finished stitching, tie the yarn end in a double knot and trim the excess. Cut a piece of yarn and tie it into a bow at the top of the plastic canvas.

SAFE CAPE

344

Dressing up in costumes isn't just for Halloween—it's for any time you want to have a blast!

What You'll Need: 1 yard of fabric, yardstick, scissors, 14 inches of elastic, sewing machine, fabric paints (optional)

Have an adult help you with this project. Cut a triangle of fabric about 30 inches long and 30 inches wide at the bottom. Cut off the tip so that the new edge is 7 inches long. Cut points along the bottom edge to make a bat cape. Cut the elastic in half. Sew one end of an elastic piece to the top of one corner of the cape. Measure 6 inches down the side and sew the other end of the elastic to the cape. Repeat with the second piece of elastic. If you want, decorate the cape with fabric paint. Let the paint dry. Put your arms through the elastic to wear the cape.

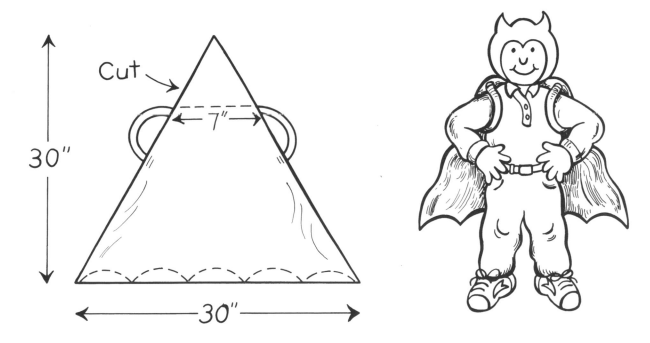

COOKIES ON A STICK

345

These cookies are as much fun to make as they are to eat.

What You'll Need: Sugar cookie dough (store-bought or homemade), food coloring, plastic bag, waxed paper, flour, cookie sheet, craft sticks

Divide the cookie dough into 3 or 4 balls. Add food coloring to each ball. Knead the dough to mix the colors. Place the dough in a plastic bag and chill in the refrigerator for an hour. Cover your work surface with waxed paper and sprinkle it with a bit of flour. Roll a piece of dough into a round pancake. Then roll pieces of dough into balls and strips. Use the strips and balls of dough to add features on the pancake. Make funny faces or animal characters. Place the cookies on a cookie sheet. Insert a craft stick into the bottom edge of each cookie. With an adult's help, bake the cookies following the package or recipe directions.

PAINT-A-PATCH

346

Show your school spirit or your dedication to a cause by designing a patch that sends a message.

What You'll Need: Denim fabric, pencil, fabric paint, scissors, needle and thread

Draw a circle or square on the denim fabric with a pencil. Sketch in a design on the circle or square. It can be a team logo, a rain forest scene, or a pretty picture. Use fabric paint to fill in the design. Put an outline of fabric paint around the circle or square. Let the paint dry. Have an adult cut out the patch. With an adult's permission, sew the patch on your T-shirt, jacket, or jeans.

WAITING KIT

347

No more boring waiting rooms with nothing interesting to do. This project creates activities for you to do anytime, anywhere.

What You'll Need: 10×24-inch piece of muslin, needle and thread, yarn or string, cardboard, permanent markers or fabric paint

THE WAITING KIT

Hem the 2 short ends of muslin. Fold the muslin in half bringing the 2 hemmed ends together with the hems facing out. Have an adult cut a few small holes in the hemmed ends for the drawstring. Thread a piece of yarn or string through the holes and tie it in a knot. Sew the 2 side seams closed. Turn the bag inside out. Place a piece of cardboard inside the bag. Decorate the bag with permanent markers or fabric paint. Let the paint dry. Remove cardboard. Fill the bag with a notepad, colored pencils, crayons, scissors, a glue stick, a travel game, and a good book.

SILLY PHOTOS

348

Create silly stories about your friends with pictures of them in all sorts of outrageous situations.

What You'll Need: Camera, color film, tape measure, blunt scissors, craft glue, poster board

Take pictures individually of 5 or 6 friends all standing like they have their arm around an imaginary friend's shoulder. Take each photo from a different distance: 3, 5, 7, 9, and 12 feet away. Once the photos are developed, cut out the pictures of your friends. Arrange the individual photos together in a mixed-up order to make one group picture. Glue the group photo on the poster board.

If you want, make more silly photos. Find magazine pictures of background scenes or vehicles such as mountains or the space shuttle. Glue cutout photos of your friends into the picture.

CREWEL BURLAP

349

Artwork can be drawn with pen, pencil, or paint, but it can also be drawn with yarn.

What You'll Need: Craft burlap (available at craft or fabric stores), markers, assorted colors of yarn, needlepoint needle

Draw a picture on the burlap with markers. Make a picture of a garden with a scarecrow and a split-rail fence with a line of crows. Following the outline, sew yarn around your picture in long and short stitches. Go in and out with needlepoint needle using different colors of yarn to match what you are outlining. You can even fill in areas by going back and forth with the yarn. Pick small areas to fill in that need emphasizing in your picture such as the black crows and the scarecrow's face.

EDIBLE SCULPTURE

350

Watch everyone ooh and ahh when you bring your bread sculpture to the dinner table.

What You'll Need: Loaf of frozen bread dough, waxed paper, butter knife, cookie sheet

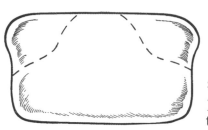

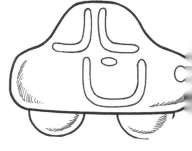

Thaw the bread dough. Cover your work surface with waxed paper. Place the dough on the waxed paper and cut into the basic loaf shape to make a car. Cut off the top 2 corners of the loaf. Knead each corner piece into a ball. Cut one ball in half and roll the halves to make the car wheels. Roll the other ball into strips to make the doors and windows. Place all the pieces on the car shape. Have an adult help you bake the dough in the oven following package directions. Let the bread cool.

STILL LIFE PHOTOGRAPHY

351

Use light and texture to tell something about what you like.

What You'll Need: Camera, black-and-white or color film, interesting objects (for the still life arrangement)

Instead of photographing people or scenes, experiment with making a still life. A still life is an arrangement of objects that have interesting shapes and textures. Artists often use strong light to make interesting shadows. Many artists arrange fruits and vases as subjects; you can try a basketball, shoes, hoop, and net or whatever else interests you. Look for some interesting objects and arrange them on a table. Take a picture of your still life arrangement. Try using different kinds of light such as natural light, spotlight, or colored light when taking your photos. Take pictures from different angles as well.

BEANBAGS

352

These soft bags can be used for target practice or a fun game of catch.

What You'll Need: ⅔ yard of fabric, scissors, needle and thread, stuffing materials such as dried beans, aquarium rocks, or small packing peanuts

Have an adult cut three 4×8-inch pieces of fabric. Fold them in half vertically to form a square. Sew two sides closed on each square of fabric. At the open end, fill the squares with stuffing materials. Make them heavy or light, depending on how you will use the beanbags. To make heavy bags, use aquarium rocks; to make light bags, use packing peanuts; to make medium-weight bags, use dried beans. Sew the last side closed. Use the bags to play the Beanbag Games on page 125.

 # WEAVING FRAME

353

With your frame, you can weave one square for a pot holder or weave lots of squares for a rug.

What You'll Need: Four 1×2-inch wood boards, saw, sandpaper, pencil, ruler, forty-six 1-inch nails, hammer, wood glue, C-clamps, cotton string, crochet hook, yarn, wide-tooth comb or pick, blunt scissors

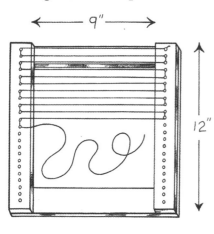

Have an adult saw two 12-inch pieces and two 9-inch pieces from the wood boards. Make sure you sand the wood smooth. Use a pencil to mark 23 dots along each 12-inch wood piece about ½ inch apart. Have an adult hammer the nails in the wood at each mark. To make the frame, glue the wood pieces in a square with the 12-inch pieces on top of the 9-inch pieces (see illustration). Hold the pieces together with C-clamps, and let the frame dry overnight.

Tie the cotton string to the first nail and run the string back and forth around the nails. Tie it off at the last nail. Poke the crochet hook over and under the cross threads. Hook in the yarn and pull it through. On the next pass, go under and over. Use the comb to tighten the threads against one another. When you are finished, cut the strings and tie them off.

POINT OF VIEW PHOTO

354

With photography, you can make objects bigger than a building or smaller than a stone. It all depends on the angle.

What You'll Need: Camera, color film

Take pictures from a different angle than usual. For example, photograph your dog from a ladder, your brother from down by his feet, a nature scene from between two branches, or a group of friends from one end of the group. It's an easy thing to do, and it will give your photos a new twist. Make a study of a series of items by examining them from different angles and from close and far away.

DOLL'S BEDCLOTHES

355

Tuck your doll or stuffed animal into its own bed with a mattress, pillow, and bedspread you made yourself.

Bedspread

What You'll Need: ¾ yard of white fabric, yardstick, blunt scissors, cotton batting, needle and thread, ½ yard of print fabric, 1¼ yard of ½-inch-wide lace

Cut a 7×7-inch piece and a 13×18-inch piece of white fabric. To make the pillow, fold the small piece in half and sew two sides closed. To make the mattress, fold the big piece in half so it measures 9×13 inches. Sew two sides closed. Turn both pieces inside out. Stuff the pillow and the mattress with batting. Fold the open end on each piece under and sew it closed. For the bedspread, cut a 13×15-inch piece of print fabric. Hem the edges of the fabric and sew lace trim all around the bedspread.

Stuff

foldline

Mattress

FELT FINGER PUPPETS

356

With these finger puppets, you can put on a show with ten characters on stage all at once.

What You'll Need: Felt, fine-point markers, blunt scissors, needle and thread, yarn, craft glue

1. Trace the finger puppet pattern on a piece of felt and cut it out. Fold the piece in half at the fold line. Put the felt piece on your finger to make sure it fits. Remove the felt piece.

2. Stitch around the edges of the felt, leaving the straight end open. Turn felt inside out.

3. Draw on the puppet's eyes, nose, and mouth with fine-point markers. Glue on yarn for hair, or add cutout felt pieces for a crown, ears, or animal's mane. If you want, cut out short felt arms or paws. Glue them to the puppet right above your knuckle. When you bend your fingers, the arms will move. Make more finger puppets so you can put on a show.

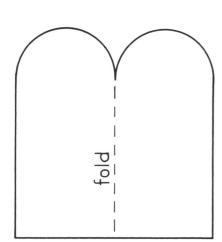

Fold fabric in half.

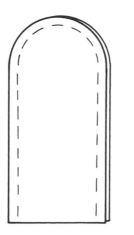

Stitch around the edges.

Decorate the felt.

FLOWER PRESS

357

With your flower press you can preserve the beauty of the season and its lovely flowers.

What You'll Need: Large piece of thin plywood, C-clamp, power drill, ¼-inch drill bit, sandpaper, blunt scissors, cardboard, construction paper, assorted flowers, four 2×¼-inch bolts, 4 wing nuts, 4 washers

Have an adult saw two 10-inch squares from the plywood. Clamp the pieces together. Have an adult drill a ¼-inch hole in each corner all the way through both boards. Unclamp the plywood pieces and sand the edges. Cut four 10-inch squares from cardboard and six 10-inch squares from construction paper. Cut the corners off each square. Place a cardboard square on top of one plywood piece and a square of construction paper on top of the cardboard. Arrange your flowers on top of the construction paper. Place a second square of construction paper on top of the flowers, then another cardboard square. Continue with additional layers of materials following the same order.

After all the layers are arranged, place the second piece of plywood on top of everything. Insert the bolts in each hole, put on the washers, and tighten down the wing nuts. Put your flower press in a warm, dry place for at least six months. The longer the flowers are allowed to dry, the less likely their color is to fade when you use them in a design.

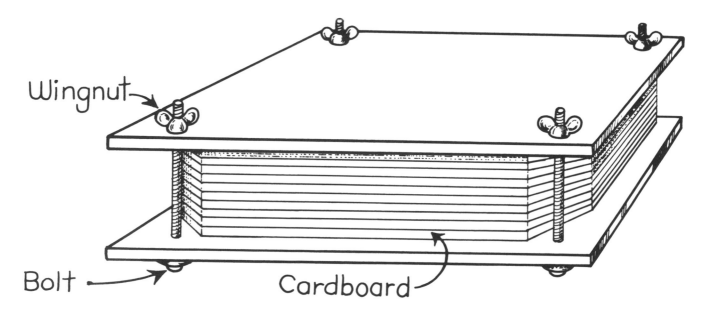

SCULPTING COOKIES

358

The dough starts out looking like real clay, but after it's baked, there's no doubt it's a sweet treat.

What You'll Need: ½ cup peanut butter, 2 tablespoons honey, 1 egg, ¾ cup flour, ½ teaspoon baking soda, mixing bowl and spoon, waxed paper, cookie sheet

Mix all the ingredients together thoroughly. Place a sheet of waxed paper on your work surface. Sprinkle a bit of flour over the waxed paper. Knead the dough on the floured waxed paper. Pinch and shape the dough just like clay. Sculpt it into a worm, snail, or ladybug, or form the dough into letters of the alphabet. Place the sculptures on an ungreased cookie sheet. Have an adult help you bake the cookies at 350 degrees Fahrenheit for 8 to 10 minutes. Let them cool.

COILED COASTERS

359

These soft coasters are remarkably sturdy, making them not only pretty to look at but useful, too.

What You'll Need: Clothesline cord, blunt scissors, tape measure, 1¾ yards of fabric, fabric glue

Cut four 54-inch pieces of clothesline cord. Cut four 1×54-inch strips of fabric. Wrap a fabric strip around one 54-inch piece of clothesline. Dot some glue along the rope to hold it. Once you reach the end of the cord, glue the end of the fabric strip in place. Start a small coil of the covered cord and use fabric glue to hold it together. Continue coiling the cord around itself. Put glue on the cord as you coil it. When you get to the end, tuck it in between the last coil. Add a dab of glue to secure it. Let it dry overnight. Repeat to make 3 more coasters.

360

PHOTO COLLAGE

You can describe a particular object with a series of photographs and never even say or write a word.

What You'll Need: Camera, color film, craft glue, long matboard (available at art supply stores)

Take a series of different photos of the same thing such as several types of dogs or close-ups of a variety of flowers. Glue the photographs in a row on a colorful piece of matboard. Choose a color that picks up something in your pictures. You can also take a series of pictures of parts of an object. For instance, take photos of car tires, the trunk of the car, and the car grille. Put them together on the matboard. Make several photo collages and have a showing of your photography.

PAINT-PROOF ART SMOCK

361

There's no need to worry about messy art projects! Put on your smock and let your imagination go wild.

What You'll Need: Measuring tape, vinyl fabric, blunt scissors, 14 inches of ¾-inch-wide elastic, needle and thread, permanent markers

Measure yourself from neck to mid-thigh and from shoulder to shoulder. Cut a long rectangle of vinyl two times as long as your body measurement and as wide as your shoulders. Cut a hole in the center for your head. Try it on and see how it fits. Mark the position of where the elastic will go from one side to the other at your waist. Cut the elastic in half. Sew each piece on the vinyl fabric. Decorate your art smock with permanent markers.

BOOK PILLOW

362

After you get home from the library, curl up with your reading pillow and dive into your books.

W h a t You'll Need: 1⅓ yards of fabric, ruler, blunt scissors, newspaper, fabric paint, fabric glue, cotton batting, bias tape, black fabric marker

1. Cut a 12×19-inch piece and a 3×28-inch piece of fabric. Cover your work surface with newspaper. Place the 12×19-inch piece of fabric on your work surface right side up. Divide the fabric as shown in the illustration for the front cover, spine, and back cover, and decorate it with fabric paint to look like your favorite book. Paint on the title and illustrations. Let the paint dry.

2. Use fabric glue to put together the seams to make the pillow. Apply a line of glue along the edges of the 3×28-inch piece of fabric. Attach one end of the 3×28-inch piece of fabric to the bottom of the spine. Continue gluing and attaching the long strip around the edges of the book fabric until you get to the top edge. Leave it open. Stuff the book with batting, then glue the last edge closed.

3. Place bias tape over the edges with more fabric glue. Draw some lines on the long strip to create the pages of the book.

glue

Glue the long strip of fabric to the book edges.

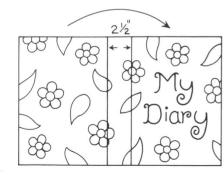

Decorate the fabric to look like your favorite book.

2½"

Draw lines on the long strip to make pages.

TEPEE

363

With your tepee you can sleep outside under the stars and pretend you're a traveler on the Great Plains.

What You'll Need: Four 1×2-inch wood boards about 4 feet long, power drill, ⅜-inch drill bit, 12 inches of cord, 2⅓ yards of muslin about 44 inches wide, scissors, fabric paint, fabric glue, needle and strong thread

1. Have an adult drill a hole 2 inches from the top of each board. Thread the cord through the holes and tie the boards together to make the tepee frame. Tie the cord in a knot. Spread the boards out to form the frame.

Tie boards together to make the tepee frame.

2. Have an adult trim one end of the muslin fabric to form a half circle. Cut a U-shape at the center of the straight edge of the muslin. Use fabric paint to decorate the muslin with a Native American design. Let the paint dry. Fold the straight end of the fabric over about 4 inches and glue a seam to make a pocket. Let the glue set.

Fold the straight end of the fabric over and glue in place.

3. Slip 2 boards of the tepee frame through the fabric pockets. The tied ends of the boards should poke through the U-shaped hole at the top. Sew a piece of thread around the center point of the 2 back boards of the tepee to hold them in place. Stand the frame up, and spread the boards out to form the tepee.

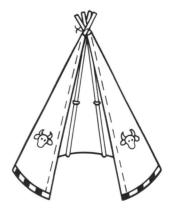

Slip the boards through the fabric pockets.

TRAFFIC SIGNS

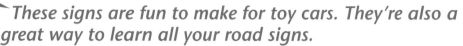

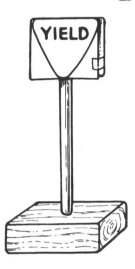

These signs are fun to make for toy cars. They're also a great way to learn all your road signs.

What You'll Need: Five 1×2-inch boards, five ¼-inch wood dowels, saw, sandpaper, power drill, ¼-inch drill bit, tape measure, wood glue, cardboard, blunt scissors, markers, transparent tape

Have an adult saw and drill all the wood pieces. Make sure you sand the wood smooth. Saw the 1×2-inch boards into 2-inch pieces for the base of the signs. Drill a ¼-inch hole in the center of each wood base. Saw the dowels into 4-inch pieces for the sign posts. Glue each dowel in a base.

To make a sign, cut a 4×1½-inch piece from the cardboard. Fold it in half and draw a traffic sign on both sides. Tape the sides closed to make a pocket. Slip it over a dowel sign post. Repeat to make 4 more signs. For instance, you could make a stop sign, yield sign, traffic signal, railroad crossing, or a walk/don't walk sign.

CANDY APPLE CREATURES

An apple a day keeps the doctor away, but an apple creature keeps your friends smiling.

What You'll Need: Waxed paper, apples, caramel apple wrappings (available at grocery stores), assorted candies such as gumdrops, candy corn, and licorice, craft sticks

Cover your work surface with waxed paper. Wrap an apple with a sheet of caramel. Turn the apple upside down. Make a funny face on the caramel apple. Use gumdrops for the eyes, candy corn for the teeth, and licorice for the hair. Insert a craft stick in the apple. Tie a piece of licorice around the craft stick to make a bow. Make more silly characters with red hots, popcorn, or chocolate chips.

INDEX